SMALL FAMILY GARDENS

For Mitzi, CiCi & Kitty

Published in Great Britain in 2007 by John Wiley & Sons Ltd

Copyright © 2007
John Wiley & Sons Ltd, The Atrium, Southern Gate, Chichester,
West Sussex PO19 8SQ, England
Telephone (+44) 1243 779777

Email (for orders and customer service enquiries): cs-books@wiley.co.uk
Visit our Home Page on www.wiley.com

Other Wiley Editorial Offices

John Wiley & Sons Inc., 111 River Street, Hoboken, NJ 07030, USA

Jossey-Bass, 989 Market Street, San Francisco, CA 94103-1741, USA

Wiley-VCH Verlag GmbH, Boschstr. 12, D-69469 Weinheim, Germany

John Wiley & Sons Australia Ltd, 42 McDougall Street, Milton, Queensland 4064, Australia

John Wiley & Sons (Asia) Pte Ltd, 2 Clementi Loop #02-01, Jin Xing Distripark, Singapore 129809

John Wiley & Sons Canada Ltd, 5353 Dundas Street West, Suite 400, Etobicoke, Ontario M9B 6H8

Wiley also publishes its books in a variety of electronic formats. Some content that
appears in print may not be available in electronic books.

Executive Commissioning Editor: Helen Castle
Executive Project Editor: Amie Tibble
Content Editor: Louise Porter
Publishing Assistant: Calver Lezama

ISBN 978 0 470 06555 6

Cover Photograph © Juliette Wade

Anniversary Logo Design: Richard Pacifico

Design and layouts by Jeremy Tilston, The Oak Studio Limited
Printed and bound by Conti Tipocolor, Italy

SMALL FAMILY GARDENS

Caroline Tilston

Photography
Juliette Wade

John Wiley & Sons Ltd

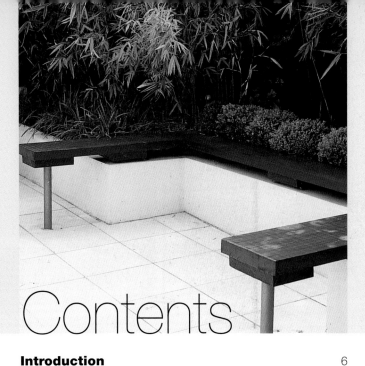

Contents

Introduction

'The garden is the last luxury of our day and age, because it is rooted in the very aspects of our lives that have become most rare and precious: time, care, and space.'

Dieter Kienast

Gardens are a luxury. Of course you can live without one, but if you do have one what a wonderful opportunity it is – an opportunity to have fun, to make a connection with nature and to create your own world. Although they're a luxury, gardens are incredibly important. In many ways the more busy you are, the more important they become: a moment watching a bird or a few minutes digging in the soil can be a tonic to all the 'white noise' of modern life.

Gardens are our own bit of the world: we can mould them and create something entirely to our own taste. Just look at the gardens in this book. Each one is unique and each reflects the needs and style of its owners.

Gardens do this in a way that any room inside the house can't. Outside you aren't limited by four walls and a ceiling. You create your walls, your ceiling – you make your space. There's also greenery and nature, a chance to hide away and escape.

These things that are so wonderful for adults are even more essential for children and it really pays to put some thought into your garden after becoming a parent. I think most people have childhood memories of grass and dens, of worms and dirt. Gardens are where children can really be children. In the past we may have wandered about the streets or fields, but now children are confined to their gardens because of fears for their safety, so the garden has become the one place where they can roam free.

The hugely important needs of both adults and children are what define a family garden. Adults want to relax and perhaps create a wonderful space. Children want to play and … enjoy a wonderful space. As soon as you start to spell them out you realise that these needs don't necessarily have to be competing. What's exciting to an adult is exciting to a child and certainly, with a little thought, adults and children can enjoy the same space and you can create a real family garden. Whether it's a social space, a place to eat or a place to have fun, the garden can provide what you need.

This joint adventure, this delight in the outside space, is what is really new and exciting in gardens right now – this is what defines a modern garden. Adults are realising that much more is possible outside than in and much more is possible in the garden than we even considered five or ten years ago. And the adventure is for adults and children alike. A den can work as a place to escape for adults as well as children. Even just a hammock, wonderful for adults to lie on, becomes a pirate ship when a few kids climb up into it. Coloured lights are enchanting for everyone – the list goes on. There are so many things that children and adults can both appreciate. Good design, exciting design, is something that everyone can enjoy.

And for once, size really doesn't matter. All of the gardens in this book are small, but each one is different and each one is magical. Children are small too, and they find smaller gardens less daunting. For adults equally, a small garden can be just right: it's the worst thing to feel that you can't enjoy your garden because there's too much to do in it. A small garden can be a complete pleasure – enough gardening to feel mud on your hands, but not so much that you feel lead in your heart.

This book

Most people don't actually read gardening books, at least not from cover to cover. In fact, if you've got this far you're unusual and I thank you.

What people do do is look at the pictures and read the information they need to find out. I know that time is short and gardening books sometimes forget their main place: as reference books. This is a reference book so I've tried to make the information as easy to access, as lively and as interesting as possible ... and the pictures are pretty nice too.

The gardens

The gardens in this book range from incredibly natural to sleekly modern. As an exercise in seeing what can be done with what were previously bog-standard back gardens, they are wonderful to look at and a real testament to the ingenuity of the people who shaped them.

So what's in this book?

- The book features 14 gardens, ranging from the absolutely tiny to a 'normal'-sized back garden.

- It is packed with information on each garden, so whether you want to recreate the whole look or just elements from it, you can be inspired by the gardens – it's up to you to take that inspiration and make it a reality.

- With each garden I talk about its design and the plants in it and pick out a feature, like creating a pond or growing vegetables, and give more 'how to' information about it.

- There are step-by-step guides to garden projects.

- The design details of every garden are included along with plans and annotated pictures to explain each of the garden designs.

- The book also gives details of relevant suppliers and products.

So you get:

- Brilliant, beautiful, contemporary design ideas especially for small gardens and families.

- Loads of information and ideas about the perfect plants for you.

- Great ideas for garden features and hands-on projects that you can do in the garden.

The layout

There are five double-page spreads for each of the 14 gardens. These are designed as follows:

1. Introduction

With a big wide shot of the garden and a little information about the brief for the design.

2. The Garden

The same picture but with important aspects of the design pulled out and annotated. Down the right-hand side are close-up pictures of the features in the garden.

3. Design

This double-page spread has a plan of the garden and a connected feature about garden design.

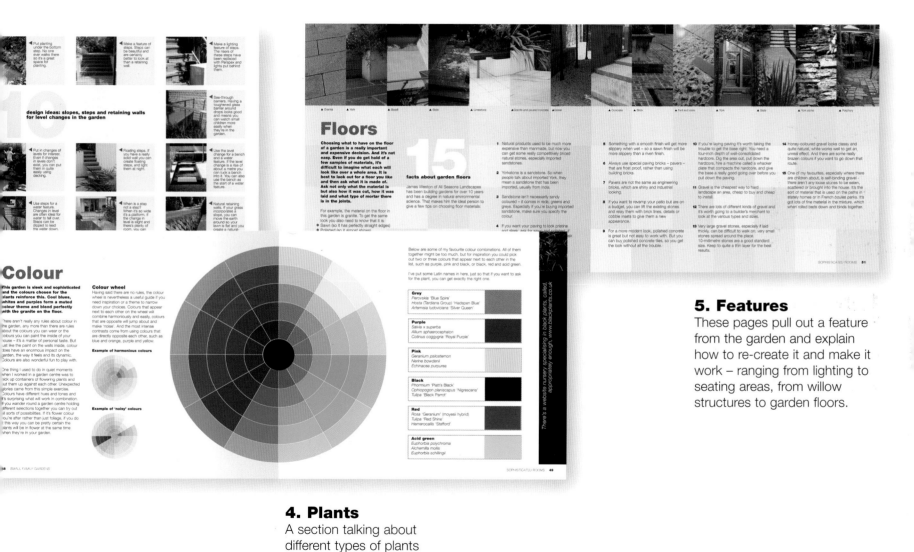

5. Features

These pages pull out a feature from the garden and explain how to re-create it and make it work – ranging from lighting to seating areas, from willow structures to garden floors.

4. Plants

A section talking about different types of plants and planting related to the garden.

So, read on and enjoy!

Minimalist

DESIGN BRIEF
- **Contemporary minimalist**
- **Stairway made safe for children**
- **Space to eat outside**

FEATURES
- **Italian basalt table**
- **Toughened glass and stainless-steel fence**
- **Slatted cedar trellis**

'In a very small space everything has to be perfect.' James Lee, the designer of this garden, is true to his word. It's a wonderful example of pared-down perfection. Everything here has a strong line and a clear purpose and all of it is beautifully executed and detailed.

The tiny space has two entrances: one from below ground, from the kitchen, and one from the living room, set slightly above the garden.

'Our priority was to make it safe for the children. Before there were all different levels and open stairs.'

Boundaries The walls are covered in cedar slatwork. Made from different thicknesses of cedar, this slatwork unifies the whole space. With the cedar on them, the walls don't need to be covered with planting; they are a part of the design and can be left bare. Held within the walls is the central, beautifully proportioned space.

Keeping it clear The garden has an empty central space. Empty because, with a tiny garden like this, James decided it was best to leave as much of the area as possible uncluttered. This makes it appear larger and allows for maximum flexibility in the way adults and children use it. So there's room for children's toys to be brought out in the daytime and then cleared away later.

Safety Small children play in this garden – the toughened glass fence protects the stairwell and as it's see-through it allows their mother to see them from inside the house. The fence is surprisingly high behind the table here, but this is so even if the children climb on the table they are protected from the stairwell.

Low-maintenance planting Black bamboo along the rear and mind-your-own-business on the ground are wonderful structural, low-maintenance plants to give greenery all year round. Only one other plant is used in the central area of the garden; this small number of plants helps to keep the design low maintenance.

Space savers The wide edge of the raised bed at the rear of the garden forms a built-in seat. There's also a built-in table, difficult to see as it's made of the same material as the floor (Italian basalt) so it blends in beautifully.

▲ **From the kitchen** steep stairs rise up to the garden. They are beautifully finished in Italian basalt with toughened glass and stainless-steel railings.

▲ **The side** of the raised bed is perfect for sitting on.

▲ **From the kitchen**, at the lower level, the view is of a trained Australian ivy, which does very well in this sheltered spot at the base of the wall.

◄**The space on the floor** between the raised bed and the line of mind-your-own-business is just right to put your feet down on without stepping on the plants. The mind-your-own-business hides the drainage for the area and benefits from the water that drains away here. It also breaks up the expanse of the floor without impinging on its use at all.

'Minimalism doesn't mean empty. I could describe this garden by saying "a small area with a long bench, a table and about 20 per cent of the area given over to plants". That could describe any garden. What's here is a precise use of line, a carefully thought-out integration of function and form and a balance to the design, which gives it stability and strength. It is so clean, so clear, that the lack of space doesn't matter; indeed, this stark minimalism wouldn't work so well in a larger garden.'

Design

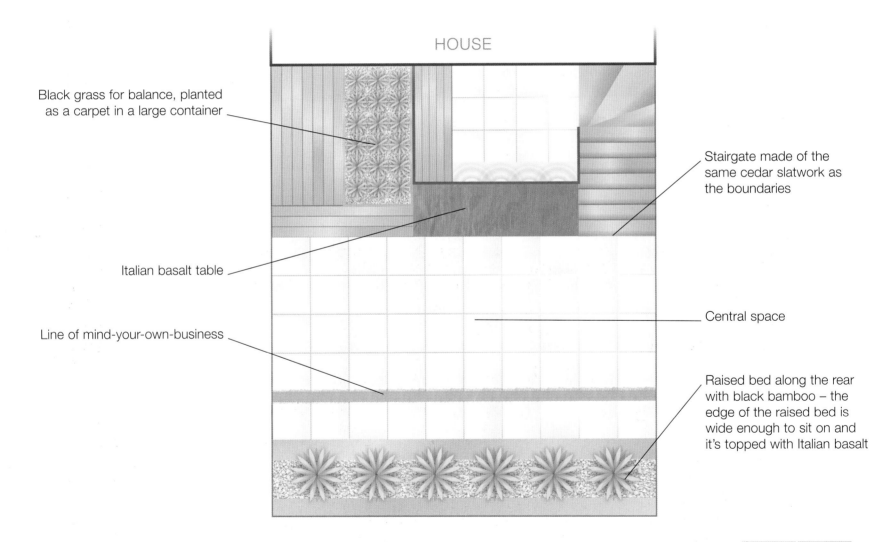

HOUSE

Black grass for balance, planted as a carpet in a large container

Italian basalt table

Line of mind-your-own-business

Stairgate made of the same cedar slatwork as the boundaries

Central space

Raised bed along the rear with black bamboo – the edge of the raised bed is wide enough to sit on and it's topped with Italian basalt

0   0.5   1 metres.

Making minimalism: Creating a minimalist garden

Minimalist gardens aren't easy to get right. There's no fudging around the edges, no room for a slight mistake; what is there has to be spot on. But on the plus side, they tend to be low maintenance and a tranquil antidote to our busy lives. With their roots in the Orient, minimalist gardens are places for contemplation and repose. As Shunmyo Masuno says in the introduction to *The Modern Japanese Garden*, such gardens offer 'a space that provides the means for the mind to become acutely sensitive to the simple small matters that are often blanketed by daily life'.

design tips for a minimalist garden

1. Remove all unnecessary components and decorations from the design. The elements must be 'condensed to the essentials', as architect John Pawson says. He goes on, 'One of the most significant principles is to omit the unimportant, in order to emphasise the important.'

2. With what you have left, make a clear, strong, simple composition.

3. Think not only about what's going in but also about the spaces left in between.

4. A composition that uses sharp geometry and highly structured forms is key. Mathematically ideal forms, spheres, cubes, cones and pyramids have calmness and harmony.

5. Although minimalist doesn't have to mean symmetrical, symmetry gives an instant order to the design. As Magnus Enquist and Anthony Arak explain in a 1994 article in the journal *Nature* entitled 'Symmetry, beauty and evolution', humans are biologically predisposed to symmetry. Perhaps originally a survival mechanism, this propensity has transferred itself into our preferences in art and our environment.

6. Repetition in the design will provide simplicity and rhythm, which give a further ordering to the elements in the garden.

7. When you have worked out what's going where, unify and simplify the materials you are using. There are no rules for this, but for instance in this garden there are only two basic materials: Italian basalt is used for all the hard landscaping and cedar wood for the upright features.

8. Minimalist gardens are often linked to the use of modern materials to give a sleek, clean line. But look at the wonderful minimalism of Japanese gardens and you realise that natural materials can fit with the principles just as well.

9. Your selection of plants should be limited too. A jungle or cottage effect is not going to reinforce the simplicity you're looking for. The planting may even consist only of a single plant, displayed to be appreciated for its form rather than for its effect among other plants.

Books on minimalism

The best book on minimalist gardens is *The Minimalist Garden* by Christopher Bradley-Hole (Mitchell Beazley, 2005). On minimalist architecture and minimalism in general, try *Minimum* by John Pawson (Phaidon Press, 2005). On Japanese gardens take a look at *The Modern Japanese Garden* by Michiko Rico Nose (Tuttle Publishing, 2005).

▲ Perennial planting   ▲ Mind-your-own-business   ▲ Hostas   ▲ Black grass   ▲ Box bushes

Easy plants

Q What makes a low-maintenance plant?

A. A plant that suits the conditions and the site. It sounds simple enough, but putting a shade-loving plant in the sun or a plant that grows huge in small space is going to create more work.

● Something that will forgive a little neglect, especially a plant that can survive a dry spell. Most plants need a little help in their first year, but after that there are plenty that will thrive without additional water.

● A plant that's slow growing or at least well behaved, so once it reaches a good size it doesn't start to take over the garden.

● Something that looks good all year round so you can simply leave it alone.

Q What about a whole planting scheme, how can that be made low maintenance?

A. Even plants that aren't necessarily low maintenance can be included if the way the planting is designed is smart.

● If the soil is free of weeds it cuts down on the work and gives your plants the best start.

● Go for a single type of plant and use lots of it, or (as in this garden) select just two or three different types of plants.

● However many plants you choose, try to make sure they have the same requirements. For example, there are quite a few perennials that need cutting down at the same time in spring and you can do this very quickly with garden shears.

● Make sure you have easy access to the plants, so if you have to do anything you're not fighting your way in.

● Some people swear by covering the soil with black semi-permeable membrane before you do your planting. If weeds are a problem this can help, but the membrane tends to rise up at the edges and can look awful.

● One of the ways to have low-maintenance plants is to have lots of structural evergreens and just a few spaces for the higher-maintenance, 'pretty' plants.

Q So what's high-maintenance planting?

A. Something that is, for example:

● Tender – it keels over at the first sign of frost.

● Thirsty – it needs watering once or twice a day in summer.

● A plant that needs deadheading – as the flowers die, you have to remove them.

● Only around for a short time – it needs replacing or cutting down at the end of its season.

● Difficult to access.

This list pretty much sums up a hanging basket, the highest-maintenance few square inches of soil ever created by man. Hanging baskets and other containers are truly high maintenance, but because they're small, people feel in control and are happy to have them.

▲ Black elder   ▲ Bamboo   ▲ Giant feathergrass   ▲ Olive

Q Which are the best plants for a dry garden?

A. If lack of water is a problem try these plants:

Lavenders
Rosemary
Artemisia
Sea hollies
Irises
Sedums
Grasses

DESIGNER'S TIP

If you want a particular plant but can't find it, ask at a good nursery or garden centre and they may be able to get it for you, or at least suggest an alternative.

Low

Grasses These are pretty low maintenance. Choose grasses that will keep standing through the winter and you only have to see to them once a year, when you cut them down to the ground in spring. Most common forms of Miscanthus, Stipa and Molinia will work here.

Bulbs Once you've put a bulb in the ground your work is pretty much over. (I'd avoid daffodils, their leaves are too messy.) Scillas, Alliums, Camassias, snowdrops and cyclamens all look after themselves and come up looking good year after year.

Shrubs Old fashioned but worth thinking about for low maintenance. Something like an Oregon grape will give winter colour and spring flowers. The strawberry tree is evergreen, slow growing with strawberry-like fruit in winter. Silver bush is an evergreen low-growing silver-leaved shrub with white summer flowers.

Lowest of the low

All of the following plants are evergreen and, given a good start and some nice soil, tend to look after themselves.

Black grass This low-growing member of the lily family will slowly spread to cover an area.

Box Slow growing, box will be happy in sun or shade. Its most common cause of death is lack of water.

Bamboo Stick to *Phyllostachys* and you can pretty much leave the plant alone once it's settled.

Mind-your-own-business It will try to spread but will neatly fill any gaps in the paving.

Olive In a sheltered sunny spot olive trees are perfect year-round performers. Slow growing, they can quite happily survive a summer drought.

The more hard landscaping you have, the fewer plants, the lower the maintenance

What's on the walls?

In small gardens the walls are often by far the largest surface area and the first thing you notice. Getting the walls to look unified and in keeping with the style of the garden is key to making a good design.

1. Trellis panels hung over walls can work beautifully.

2. Battens are great for giving a modern look.

3. Sheets of waterproof plywood attached to the walls by mounting them on battens and then painting them can give a really clean, clear look to the garden.

4. Rendering walls can lighten up the area and the render can then be painted or left natural.

DIY DRESSING A WALL WITH BATTENS

Ingredients

- A jig if possible. You can make a batten trellis without this kind of guide, but if you're doing a whole garden it's worth making a jig up to ensure all the panels are dead straight and the same. It's basically a sheet of plywood onto which you can nail your battens as described below.

- Tanalised battens. If your battens are tanalised (treated to resist wet and rot) they'll be fine outside. It's also worth staining or painting the battens before you nail them together.

- Galvanised ring shank nails, which will stay in more securely than ordinary nails.

Step one
Knock one batten into the bottom of the jig and one a batten's length up the jig.

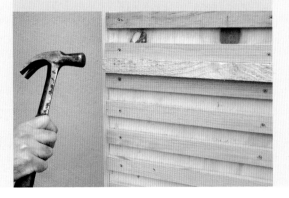

Step two
Nail in a vertical batten, making sure it's neatly tucked into the edge of the jig.

Planning permission

Usually planning guidelines limit solid boundaries to 1.8 metres high, but you can often put a 'temporary' trellis structure on top of this. It's always best to check with your local council before making any changes.

DESIGNER'S TIP

Designers often use raised beds or built-in seats to break up the height of the surrounding walls and to stop the walls dominating an area.

Step three
Put a batten alongside that one for spacing and then nail in the next one. Keep going in a hit-and-miss fashion – one for a space, one nailed in.

Step four
Pull the structure off the jig and hey presto, it's a trellis ready for fixing to your wall.

▲ This beautiful trellis, from Anthony de Grey, provides screening and enclosure around a small sitting area. Painted white, it looks more formal and urban than trellis left as plain wood.

◀ From Hillhout, an attractive way to enclose a modern garden while allowing some views out at selected points.

This great ▶ modern version of a trellis, also from Hillhout, divides the areas without cutting them off and makes an uncluttered, unfussy screen.

◀ For a less formal look this wonderfully exuberant panel from Metallic Garden provides a great screen and support for plants.

This trellis from ▶ Hillhout gives great security and safety but allows you to see through it. It's also perfect for growing plants up.

2

Mediterranean Modern

DESIGN BRIEF
- **Link with newly built house**
- **Planting that changes through the seasons**
- **A family-friendly garden**
- **Outdoor eating area**

FEATURES
- **Water feature**
- **Built-in bench**
- **Pleached pears alongside a brick wall**

What I'm going to say seems really obvious, but because it's so obvious we tend to forget it. Hard landscaping is great at providing permanent structure and definition. Soft landscaping – planting – is great at giving colour, change and life to a garden.

And although you can form strong lines with plants, the most powerful statements come from bricks and stone, concrete and render.

So at one end of the spectrum you have these unrelenting lines, and at the other planting that is diaphanous and abundant, that changes with the seasons and provides dancing informality. In this garden the two have been brought together to great effect. The design team, Tommaso del Buono and Paul Gazerwitz, have exploited these differences in shape, form and texture to create a stunning garden and proved that the most effective contrasts come from extremes.

The house sets the scene for the garden. It is a striking new build with floor-to-ceiling glass enclosed in a concrete case. All of this glass means that the views out to the garden are a major consideration. The clients wanted to see the seasons change and were inspired by Mediterranean courtyards. But they also wanted a garden that fitted with the modernism of the house.

Central tree Another tree, a Snowy Mespilus, gives height to the seating area and breaks up what would otherwise have been a solid expanse of limestone.

Limestone The same limestone is used in the garden as is used inside the house; this helps the two flow together as one area.

Planting The solution was to enclose the garden with architectural plants, formal and modern, and centrally, where perhaps a lawn might have been, to create vast beds of flowers.

Perimeter trees The trunks of trees planted at either side of the garden give a wonderful repeated pattern of uprights. On this side are strawberry trees, on the other pleached pears.

Stepping stones made from limestone run through the beds. These provide access for looking after the plants and in winter, when the planting is more sparse, they also give pattern and structure to the area.

▲ **The water feature** uses the built-in bench – a slit in the rear of the bench allows water to fall through.

▲ **Water falls** into a long narrow pool running down the side of the house, with limestone stepping stones following its line.

▲ **Pleached pears** have been used for a screen above the side wall and their trunks create a repeated vertical pattern.

▲ **The seating area** has been placed slightly away from the kitchen so the table outside and the kitchen table aren't together on either side of the glass wall.

▲ **Limestone** is a wonderful material to use here. It is reflective, light and modern, it gives an air of the Mediterranean to the area, and it also provides a foil for the brightly coloured plants.

▲ **A 'cloud'-clipped** box hedge sits along the top of the retaining wall, softening the hard lines and increasing the feeling of seclusion.

'The thing about good design is that it seems so obvious, so simple. Look at this garden and you realise that with a brief of "fitting in with the modern house but also having real planting in it", no other solution was possible. But finding that obvious solution is one of the arts of garden design. Another is to take the design idea and make it work on the ground. The proportions, the materials, the use of space all have to be right to create a garden that, like this, looks like it was meant to be.'

Design

In the centre of the back garden, where you might expect a lawn are two enormous planted beds which contrast beautifully with the clean lines of the hard landscaping around them.

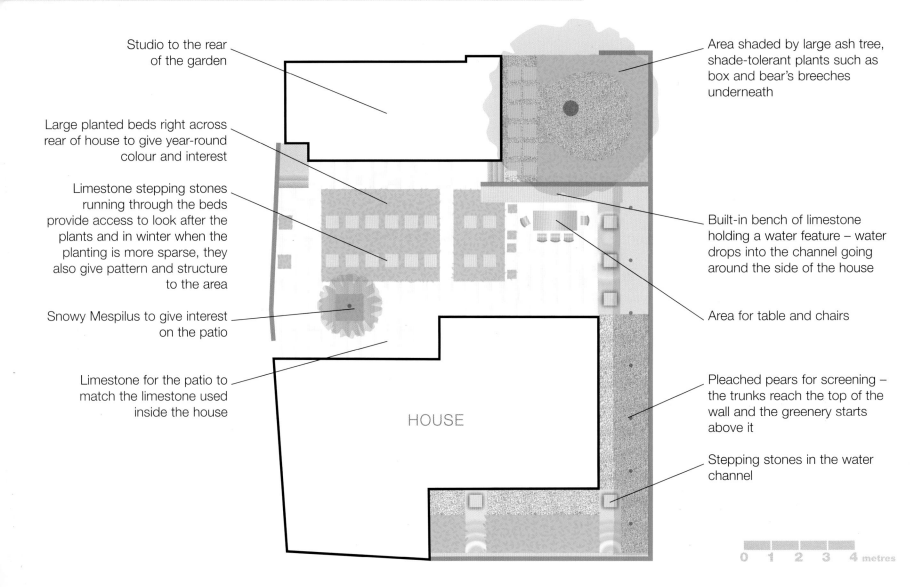

Studio to the rear of the garden

Large planted beds right across rear of house to give year-round colour and interest

Limestone stepping stones running through the beds provide access to look after the plants and in winter when the planting is more sparse, they also give pattern and structure to the area

Snowy Mespilus to give interest on the patio

Limestone for the patio to match the limestone used inside the house

Area shaded by large ash tree, shade-tolerant plants such as box and bear's breeches underneath

Built-in bench of limestone holding a water feature – water drops into the channel going around the side of the house

Area for table and chairs

Pleached pears for screening – the trunks reach the top of the wall and the greenery starts above it

Stepping stones in the water channel

HOUSE

0 1 2 3 4 metres

Employing a garden designer

It's often difficult to see how you can get the garden you want when you're used to what you have because you live with it every day. A fresh eye – a professional eye – can help. You may just need someone for a one-off consultation to get you started or to sort out a specific problem. Or at the other end of the scale, you may want someone to provide a structure and planting plans, to oversee the work and to be involved in the ongoing development of the garden.

Selecting a designer

- The best form of recommendation is personal, especially if you see a garden that the designer has already done.

- Good local nurseries will know designers working in the area and should be able to point you to one who will suit your needs.

- Garden designers often exhibit or have stands at gardening shows, national ones like the Chelsea Flower Show or local and regional shows. This is a good way of meeting several designers at one go.

- Most designers have websites that not only show pictures of their work but also reflect their style and approach.

DESIGNER'S TIP

Hard landscaping and manpower are usually the most expensive parts of building a garden. The more hard landscaping you have, the more expensive the garden will be.

Meeting the designer

The purpose of the first meeting is for the designer to have an initial look at the garden and to talk about what your needs are. The designer will be getting information to start the design process and you will be assessing whether the designer is right for you.

Assuming you've chosen an experienced designer whose style you like, communication is the next most important thing: are they listening to you and do they understand what you want? If you don't 'click' at this first meeting it may be better to find someone else. It's important that the designer leads you through the process and, even at this early stage, talks to you about the options available to achieve what you want.

After this meeting the designer will give you a quote for the design work you've discussed. They may also charge a fee for the initial meeting.

Costs

Exactly when an overall budget is talked about varies. If you know how much you want to spend, it's better to tell the designer at the start. They can then tailor their designs to this figure. If you aren't working to a specific budget you can wait until the quotes come in for the building work and then, if necessary, remove some items or trade down on materials.

Brief

Either before you start or after the first meeting, it's worth writing out a brief for the designer. This might include:

- All the things you don't like about your existing garden and any problems you've noticed.
- Any good features or plants in the garden you'd like to enhance.
- How many people (including children) are in the house.
- Whether you need to make special provision for pets or children.
- What features you would like in the new garden – water features, lighting or ornaments.
- Any other requirements that the garden has to achieve, such as sitting areas. And if there do need to be seating areas, where they should be and how many people need to be accommodated.
- Any particular plants you want or ones you really don't like.
- Any particular style you would like or other gardens you've seen that you want to draw inspiration from.
- Maintenance – how keen on gardening are you?
- Other features you may want or need to include, such as vegetable areas, bins, washing lines and compost heaps.

Trees for small gardens

If you have a small garden, don't assume trees will be too big for it. Small trees give height and screening and take up little room at ground level. There are some to avoid, however. Don't plant huge ones, obviously; some are too garish; and purple-leaved trees can be overbearing through the summer and cast too dense a shade. If you're worried about the root run of a tree near the house, plant the tree in a container – this will limit its size, but that's not necessarily a bad thing.

Lines of trees can look stunning, whether they're in containers as in this garden or in the ground – or you can plant three trees together in groups to make interesting patterns with their stems.

Flowering cherry Cherries are great and the winter-flowering kind will provide pink flowers in mild spells through the winter.

Redbud 'Forest Pansy' A slow-growing tree with big, heart-shaped burgundy leaves and a lovely shape.

Rowan Lovely little trees with ferny foliage. The Hupeh rowan is really special. Its leaves turn red and purple in autumn and its white flowers are followed by pinky white fruits – the combination of the purple leaves and pink flowers in autumn is particularly pleasing.

Strawberry tree An evergreen with white autumn flowers and red, strawberry-like berries.

Silver birch With delicate leaves and striking white bark, these are lovely trees. But they do grow quite quickly and you'd probably have to prune a silver birch or remove it from a confined space after 15 years or so.

▲ Flowering Cherry   Redbud 'Forest Pansy' ▼

Pleached trees

Pleached trees are a 'hedge on stilts'– the trunks are kept free from branches and leaves until about 5 or 6 feet off the ground. At this point the foliage is clipped to shape like a hedge. You can buy ready-pleached trees that are shaped onto a frame or you can pleach trees yourself by tying the branches in to a framework.

▲ Break up the soil at the bottom of the hole

▲ Wrong way round

▲ Right way round

▲ Put the soil back in the hole – and tread on it!

HOW TO PLANT A TREE OR SHRUB

It ain't rocket science, but there are a few things to remember when you're planting a tree or shrub.

- Dig a hole and place the plant, in its container, in the hole to make sure the hole is deep enough.

- When it is deep enough, loosen the soil at the bottom of the hole to help the roots get in.

- Place the tree or shrub (still in its container) in the hole and step back to see if it looks good. Plants tend to have fronts and backs, so make sure the best side is facing forward.

- Once you're happy, take the tree or shrub out of its container, replace it in the hole and put back all the soil around it. The next two steps are really important.

- Stand on the soil all around the tree or shrub to really firm it in. Not doing this is the most common reason for plants not doing well: people tend to be too gentle with them. My old head gardener used to go around after the other gardeners and try to pull plants out – if he could, he said they weren't planted properly. If the soil isn't firm there will be air pockets around the roots, which is the equivalent of being left dangling out of the soil.

- Water the tree or shrub really well. Not only will this give the plant water (obviously), it will help to close up any more gaps in the soil.

Some people stake trees, others don't. I don't unless the tree is really big and would be dangerous if it fell over. But most trees that go into gardens are 6 or 7 feet high and aren't really top heavy. The movement of the wind helps to strengthen their trunks and their roots. If you do stake the tree, do it low down, use a spacer on the tie so the stake doesn't cut into the bark, and check regularly to make sure the tree hasn't outgrown the tie.

When can you plant? With a tree or shrub in a pot you can plant any time as long as it's not extremely cold or hot, and as long as the plant will get watered once it's in place, by rain or by you.

How close can trees be planted? Look at a beech hedge – these are beech trees planted a foot apart.

Relax: Seating areas and furniture

There aren't any rules about seating areas in gardens, but here are some things to think about.

10 tips for seating areas

1 **Sun or shade?** In a small garden there might only be room for one seating area, so you may have to choose between sun or shade. One way to look at it is if you put the seating area in the sun, you can always bring in shade. On the other hand, if children are going to use the hard surface to play on, you may want them in complete shade.

2 **Size** How many people do you need to accommodate? And what do you want to use the area for? If it's for a table and chairs, the size of your table will often determine how large the seating area is. It's a good idea to measure around your table and chairs, but place the chairs as if they're being used and don't forget, people need to walk around the back of chairs. Obviously, built-in seating will save space.

3 Scale The size of the seating area will also be influenced by the size of the garden – the two should be similar in scale. If the seating is going to be a very dominant feature, go the whole hog and make yours a garden around a seating area.

4 Hard landscaping or grass? It is possible to have a seating area on grass, but wet weather and sinking table legs usually mean people opt for hard landscaping of some sort.

5 Surrounds A 'floating' seating area almost always looks awful. It's important to bed the seating into the garden by putting plants all around it, so you create atmosphere and seclusion. If the area is right next to a fence or wall, make sure there's some planting or at least a row of containers alongside the wall.

6 Access You will need access to the area in summer and possibly in winter, especially if children are using it. Paths will help stop too much wear and tear on grass.

7 Shape If the area has a really straightforward design with no awkward corners, not only will it be easier to lay, it will look better too.

8 Materials As few different materials as possible is usually the answer, and if you can tie them in with the house or the flooring the area will immediately become more at one with its surroundings.

9 Lighting Lighting in a seating area can look great and will mean that it can be used later and longer. If you have good lighting then even in winter, children might want to play outside into the evening.

Heating

Patio heaters do a wonderful job of heating an enclosed area but are notorious for spewing out greenhouse gases. In just two hours, a patio heater belches out about as much as the average car does per day. Instead, it's possible to get hold of firepits and chimineas that are fairly safe to use around children.

10 Plants Plants will help to give character, colour and form to the seating area. And if used within it they will help to break up what might be a large expanse of paving. There are several ways to introduce planting into seating areas:

- Leaving planting pockets in paving or cutting holes in decking for plants, shrubs or trees to grow through will liven up the area. But make sure the pockets aren't where tables and chairs need to go.
- Containers can introduce a vertical element as well as greenery.
- Scoop out some of the mortar from the floor joints when it's laid – this encourages dirt to settle and then low-growing plants to colonise the gaps between the stones.

Look where the evening sun is and put a seat there. The last drops of sunshine are often the most precious, especially if you've got children and/or are at work all day.

3

Jungle

DESIGN BRIEF
- **A city oasis**
- **Green in summer and winter**
- **Screening from neighbours**
- **Access to studio at rear of garden**

FEATURES
- **Chequerboard pattern**
- **Black basalt water feature**
- **Wide steps up to main garden**

The garden here was small, overgrown and neglected when Debbie Roberts and Ian Smith from the garden design company Acres Wild first saw it. What's more, the garden was about to shrink. The owners were building an extension out from the house and were planning a studio for the far end. What was left measured only 5.5 metres by 10 metres.

Not only was the space small, there was another challenge: a steep change in level from the entrance up to the main part of the garden. Unusually, the main way into the garden is from the basement kitchen and the ground rises by over a metre from here as you move into the garden. So a forbidding wall could have been the main view from the kitchen.

Water feature
The black basalt cube water feature fits perfectly with the chequerboard design of the garden.

No lawn The garden has lots of greenery, but no lawn.

Jungle planting Large-leaved plants hide the sides of the garden and create a lush green oasis, while the changing seasons are marked with deciduous trees such as the Japanese maple (*Acer palmatum* 'Fireglow').

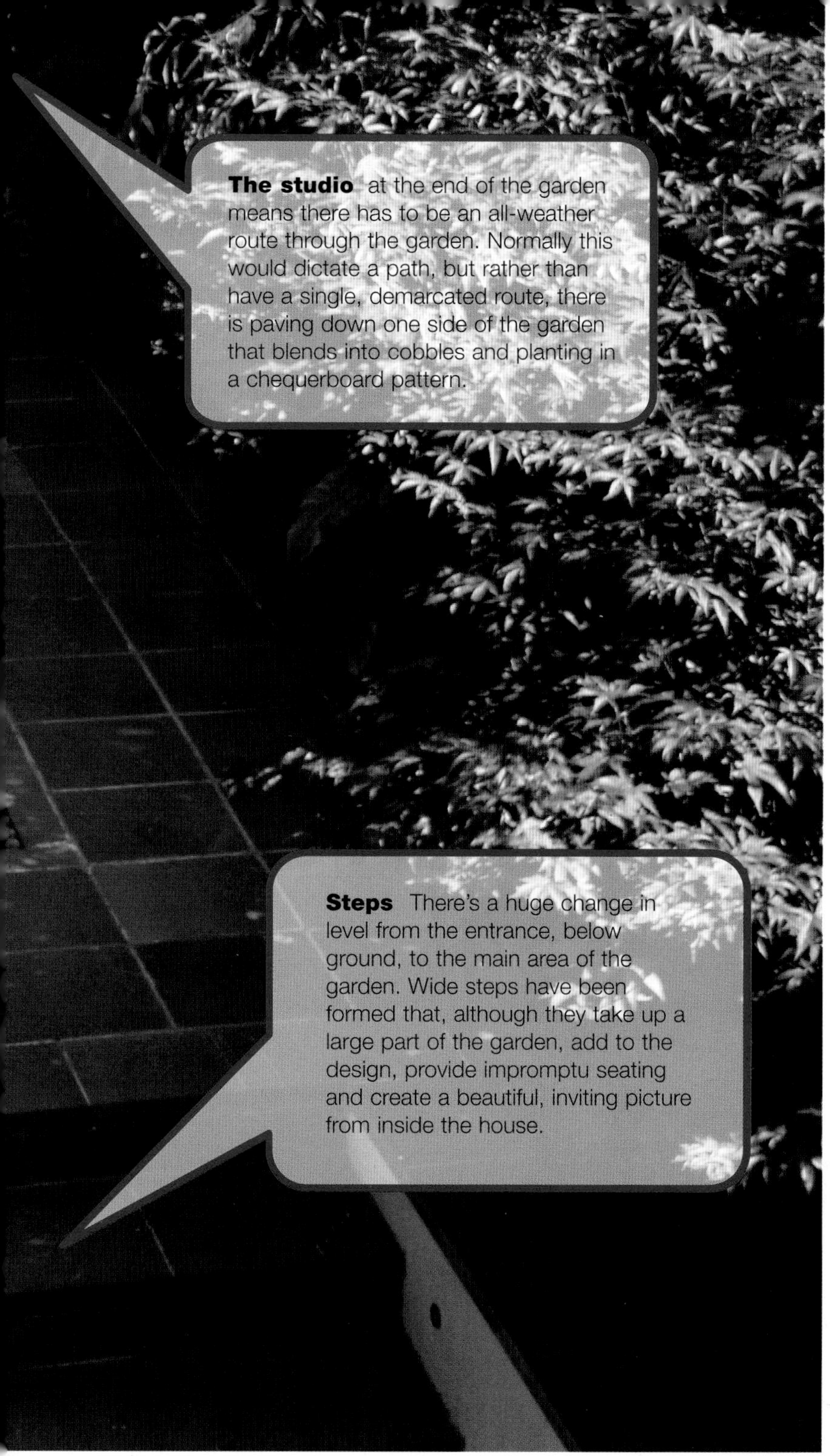

The studio at the end of the garden means there has to be an all-weather route through the garden. Normally this would dictate a path, but rather than have a single, demarcated route, there is paving down one side of the garden that blends into cobbles and planting in a chequerboard pattern.

Steps There's a huge change in level from the entrance, below ground, to the main area of the garden. Wide steps have been formed that, although they take up a large part of the garden, add to the design, provide impromptu seating and create a beautiful, inviting picture from inside the house.

▲ **Cumbrian Kirkstone** slate squares with cobbles form part of the chequerboard theme.

▲ **The Italian basalt cube** water feature is safe, robust and fun for the children.

▲ **Halfway down the garden** is a quiet place for a seat, surrounded by bamboos and arum lilies.

▲ **From the kitchen the main** view is of the wide steps, and very little can be seen of the retaining wall to either side. If the steps were narrower more of the wall would be seen and the view would have been much less inviting.

◀ **Part of the pattern of squares and cubes.** Squares on the ground made from mind-your-own-business and cobbles. Cubes made from the water feature and box bushes.

'The combination of intimate design and lush planting is essential to fulfilling a major part of the brief: to create a secluded oasis, screened from neighbours. Plants crowd in to create not just screening but atmosphere. They hide the boundaries of the garden so that its size (or lack of it) is indistinguishable.'

Design

The plan of the garden shows its length before the studio was built at the rear and the lower patio, next to the house, was extended outward with the wide steps. The remaining area has been cleverly constructed to make a well-proportioned space around the seat.

A studio and storage area along the rear of the garden

Jungle planting to hide the side boundaries

Square patterned slate and cobbles with cubes of box

Seat nestled into side planting

Wide shallow stairs up to garden

Lower area, large enough for a table and chairs

Entrance to kitchen

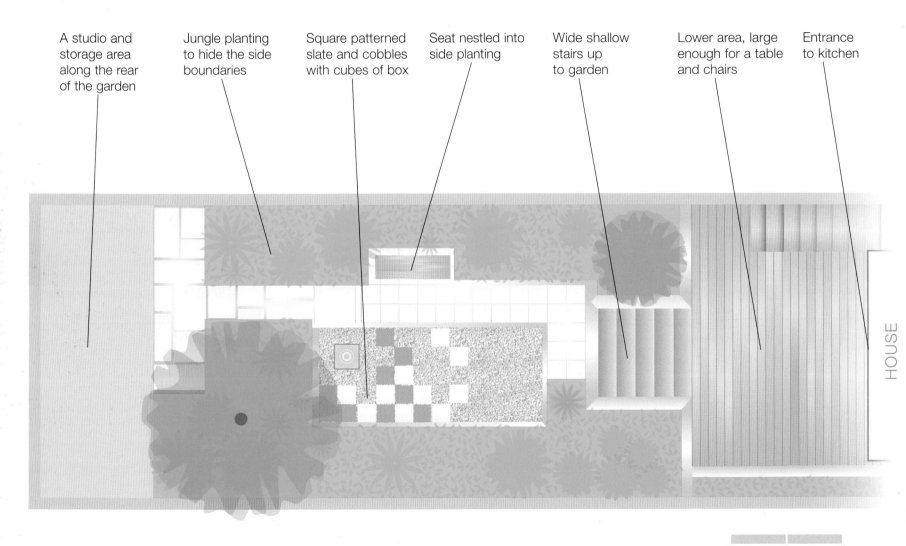

HOUSE

0   1   2 metres

To lawn or not to lawn?

In a small garden there are definite disadvantages to having a lawn, but on the other hand...

In favour of lawns in small gardens

- They're a relatively cheap way to cover ground – for the price of a handful of seed you can solve the problem of what to put in the garden.
- Compared to other planting lawns are, on the whole, lower maintenance.
- Lawns are nice to lie on and children love to play on them. It's hard to practise handstands on concrete.
- They give year-round greenery, a very important factor in the city in the middle of winter.

Against lawns in a small garden

- You need somewhere to store a lawnmower. Having sufficient storage for a lawnmower can be quite an imposition in a small garden. Also just getting the lawnmower out for a tiny area can be a bind (or am I just exceptionally lazy?).
- Lawns suffer lots of wear and tear. In a small area a lawn can get worn quite quickly because of the density of traffic.
- Small gardens are often quite shady and lawns tend not to like dark areas.
- Compared to decking or stone, lawns are high maintenance.
- When there's a lawn you immediately have a large flat surface, usually dead centre in the garden – not necessarily a bad thing, but it does restrict the design possibilities.
- In very dry summers lawns bake and go brown, in very wet winters they become impassable. Access across the lawn can be a real problem in winter.
- Children can't ride bikes on a lawn or play in soggy winter weather.
- Lawns invite no wildlife into the garden, while the right planting might.

Just looking at the number of points there's more to be said against having a lawn, but life is rarely so simple and especially if you have children there is a natural draw towards having grass.

However, it might be worth looking at artificial grass, which solves some but not all of the problems.

Is this real or fake?

The grass in this garden is Lazy Lawn™ by Evergreens UK Limited

Answer=fake

▲ Black grass   Mind-your-own-business ▼   ▼ Black bamboo   ▲ Spanish dagger   ▼ Bush ivy

9

low-maintenance, evergreen plants for creating a city jungle

These are the sorts of plants you can put in and leave alone. For the first year you can help them get established with extra water in dry spells, but otherwise they look after themselves.

▲ Chusan palm

BIG PLANTS

1 Bamboos Bamboos are happy in sun or light shade and come in many forms, but for low maintenance the best are the ones that don't spread too far, too fast. The most popular must be *Phyllostachys nigra* with black stems and *Phyllostachys aurea* with golden stems. For more leaves and less stem try *Fargesia murielae*.

2 Bush ivy Huge leaves and an ability to grow in the shadiest places make this a wonderful choice for city gardens.

3 Chusan palm This is a great hardy palm, the one to go for if you're not a gardener.

MEDIUM PLANTS

4 Oregon grape Oregon grapes have a bad reputation, being seen as 'supermarket' planting, but they will put up with most conditions. Their glossy, spiky, evergreen leaves fit well with jungle planting.

5 Spanish dagger These are best planted in full sun where the sharp rigid leaves make a strong statement and can cast wonderful shadows on walls or floors.

6 New Zealand flax These have sword-like leaves from a central base. Some are a little garish, but the new (almost) black-leaved variety, *Phormium* 'Platt's Black', is wonderful and a great foil for lighter plants.

SMALL PLANTS

7 Black Grass This short, grass-like plant comes in a lovely deep black and can be used to mirror the black *Phormium* described above. It can take its time to get established, so either buy lots or be patient.

8 Elephants' ears You have to be a little careful with elephants' ears – they are ground cover plants that flower in late winter, but some of them are truly elephantine and ugly. But try the one called 'Bressingham Ruby', whose dark purple leaves are beautiful.

9 Mind-your-own-business This is a low-growing plant that will spread along cracks in paving, forming a lovely green mat.

10 tips for water in the garden

Water adds another dimension to any garden. When it's still it has calming, reflective qualities; when it moves it gives life, light and sound to the garden.

1 Lighting the water feature can give a lot of added pleasure, especially if it's near the house. Lighting from under the water is much better than spotting a beam across its surface, which will just highlight any rubbish on the top.

2 There are two types of water feature – the ones you can buy 'off the shelf' and those that are made specially for your garden. The former are, usually, cheaper than the latter.

3 Think about what you would like from the water, why you want to have it at all. Perhaps it's for the sound (do you want a calm gurgle or a rushing cascade?), for reflections, for water plants, or for wildlife?

4 Answer these questions and the field narrows down. Another way to guide the choice is to ask whether you want a formal or informal feature. This will often be dictated by your ideas for the rest of the garden.

5

If you have an expanse of water, think about using stepping stones (or a bridge if you must).

7

Whichever you choose, the most successful water features work with the garden as part of the overall design and aren't just plonked on top as an afterthought.

9

Any depth of water can be dangerous for small children. One solution is to put a grille just under the surface of water; these can be cut specifically to fit your pond. But even then a theoretical risk remains and it might be better to stick to a feature without standing water if you have very small children.

6

If you want moving water you will need a power source. But if it's a closed system – and most are – you don't need a water supply, only water to top it up occasionally.

8

It is worth planning for the future. If you intend your garden to last through the whole of your family life, think about where teenagers and old folk (that's you!) might want to sit and while away an afternoon by a pond.

10

Consider where the water feature will be viewed from and what it will be seen against.

Sophisticated Rooms

DESIGN BRIEF
- **Modern courtyard**
- **Needs to be used at night so lighting is important**
- **Garden room at the rear of the garden**

FEATURES
- **Glass water feature**
- **Floating patio**
- **Oriental-style hideaway**

Gardens on slopes are always a little troublesome – small gardens on slopes are just plain difficult.

Small gardens that slope down, away from the house, are the most difficult of all. A decking platform going out above the garden is sometimes the best answer and avoids trying to build up the land to meet the house.

Looking on the bright side, at least the garden here slopes up from the house, so there wasn't a need to create a flat space out of thin air. But the garden is so small that any level changes needed to take into account the levels of the land in the neighbours' gardens on both sides. To create a useable flat space outside the house the land has been taken back. On each side there needed to be retaining walls to hold up the existing levels of the neighbouring gardens. At the rear of the patio the wall needed to be a tall and substantial one to hold back the rest of the garden.

Side walls The gardens on either side still have their slopes, so there are retaining walls to either side of the patio next to the house to hold back their gardens. These retaining walls and the wall at the rear of the patio enclose the area and have been used to help to create the feeling of a real 'outside room'.

Garden room At the rear, hidden among the foliage, is a garden hideaway, a separate room for escaping to.

Retaining wall The garden used to be on a slope, rising up away from the house. But, to make as much of it useable as possible, the change in level from front to back has now been accommodated by a retaining wall rather than a slope.

Water feature The rear retaining wall is also integral to the water feature. The feature was specially designed by Philip Nash for this garden and is made of imprinted glass, down which water flows. The pattern on the glass is picked out by uplighters at night.

Seats Built-in seats are a great space saver and look very sleek. A free-standing table and chairs that could seat six would take up the entire space, but this built-in alternative fits neatly into a corner and works with the design rather than cluttering it.

Paving The smooth granite blocks are laid in a regular way to emphasise a clean, modern look.

Steps One of the side walls has been used to hold the steps to the upper level. Designer Philip Nash says he wanted to make these so 'they raise the question "how's that done?" and they look beautiful at night'. Highlighted with blue lights set into the wall, the granite steps look as if they're floating in mid-air.

Platform The whole of this lower area is on a slightly raised 'platform' so the planting around is lower. At night lights around the platform make it appear to float.

▲ **The water feature** is intricate and forms the centrepiece to the garden. It has a patterned sheet of glass down which the water flows.

▲ **At night** lights shine up the glass of the water feature to catch on the pattern and the droplets of water.

▲ **White agapanthus** gives seasonal colour to enhance the evergreen structural planting. Earlier in the year the garden was full of purple tulips.

▲ **The planting sits** lower than the paving, which means that the soil and the bases of stems (which are rarely the best parts of a plant) cannot be seen. The wall behind is rendered with a product called Monocouche, which is very easy to use and gives a wonderfully smooth surface.

▲ **The oriental-looking** studio transforms the far end of the garden. Rather than being a utilitarian structure, this design adds to the ambiance. It is reached by crossing the garden – not the most direct route, but this journey is important to achieving the desired feeling of seclusion.

'The garden is great for older children who can sit with their friends and escape to their own room at the top of the garden, and it is of course stylish and welcoming for adults. The difficulties of the slope are forgotten now that the garden is in place; and indeed the garden would not work without the slope. Hiding the playroom up at the top gives an added feeling of escape and adventure. The raised plants in front of it can be seen to great effect from the house and the enclosed courtyard with its water feature would have not felt so enclosed and complete without its retaining walls.'

Design

To the left of the plan is the area created by excavating out the land, leaving a true 'outside room' surrounded by retaining walls. Up on the top level, to the right, the pathway makes a journey across the garden. The entrance to the studio could have been in line with the steps — easier to get to but that would have lessened the feeling of reaching a hideaway.

Sawn granite laid stretcher bond

Built-in seats and table of outdoor marine ply

Narrow-planted beds

Granite steps held by retaining side wall

Water feature – water falls from higher level down glass panel to narrow pond

Gravel path leads through garden to door

Studio at rear of garden, hidden from view behind planting

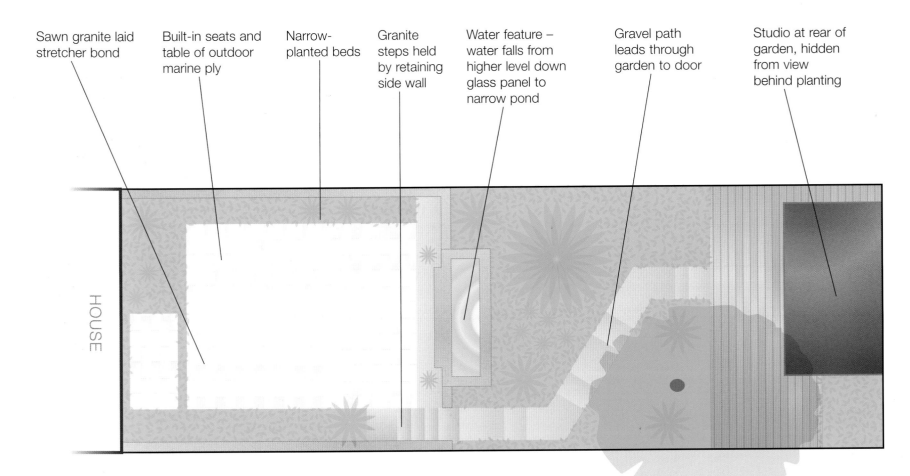

HOUSE

0   1   2 metres

◀ Put planting under the bottom step. No one ever walks there so it's a great space for planting.

◀ Make a feature of steps. Steps can be beautiful and are certainly better to look at than a retaining wall.

◀ Make a lighting feature of steps. The risers of these steps have been replaced with Perspex and lights put behind them.

10

design ideas: slopes, steps and retaining walls for level changes in the garden

◀ See-through barriers. Having a toughened glass barrier around drops looks good and means you can watch small children more easily when they're in the garden.

◀ Put in changes of levels for interest. Even if changes in levels don't exist, you can put them in quite easily using decking.

◀ Floating steps. If you have a really solid wall you can create floating steps, and light them at night.

◀ Use the level change for a bench and a water feature. If the level change is a rise of about a metre you can tuck a bench into it. You can also use the bench as the start of a water feature.

◀ Use steps for a water feature. Changes in level are often ideal for water to fall over. Steps can be dipped to lead the water down.

◀ When is a step not a step? When it's so wide it's a platform. If the change in level is slight and there's plenty of room, you can create terraces.

◀ Natural retaining walls. If your grass incorporates a slope, you can move the earth around so your lawn is flat and you create a natural-looking retaining wall to take the change in levels.

Colour

This garden is sleek and sophisticated and the colours chosen for the plants reinforce this. Cool blues, whites and purples form a muted colour theme and blend perfectly with the granite on the floor.

There aren't really any rules about colour in the garden, any more than there are rules about the colours you can wear or the colours you can paint the inside of your house – it's a matter of personal taste. But just like the paint on the walls inside, colour does have an enormous impact on the garden, the way it feels and its dynamic. Colours are also wonderful fun to play with.

One thing I used to do in quiet moments when I worked in a garden centre was to pick up containers of flowering plants and put them up against each other. Unexpected glories came from this simple exercise. Colours have different hues and tones and it's surprising what will work in combination. If you wander round a garden centre holding different selections together you can try out all sorts of possibilities. If it's flower colour you're after rather than just foliage, if you do it this way you can be pretty certain the plants will be in flower at the same time when they're in your garden.

Colour wheel

Having said there are no rules, the colour wheel is nevertheless a useful guide if you need inspiration or a theme to narrow down your choices. Colours that appear next to each other on the wheel will combine harmoniously and easily, colours that are opposite will jump about and make 'noise'. And the most intense contrasts come from using colours that are directly opposite each other, such as blue and orange, purple and yellow.

Example of harmonious colours

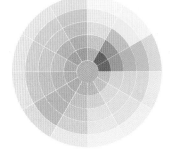

Example of 'noisy' colours

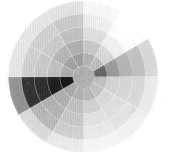

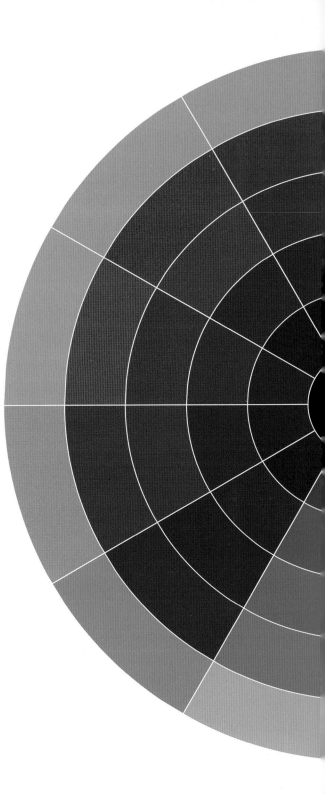

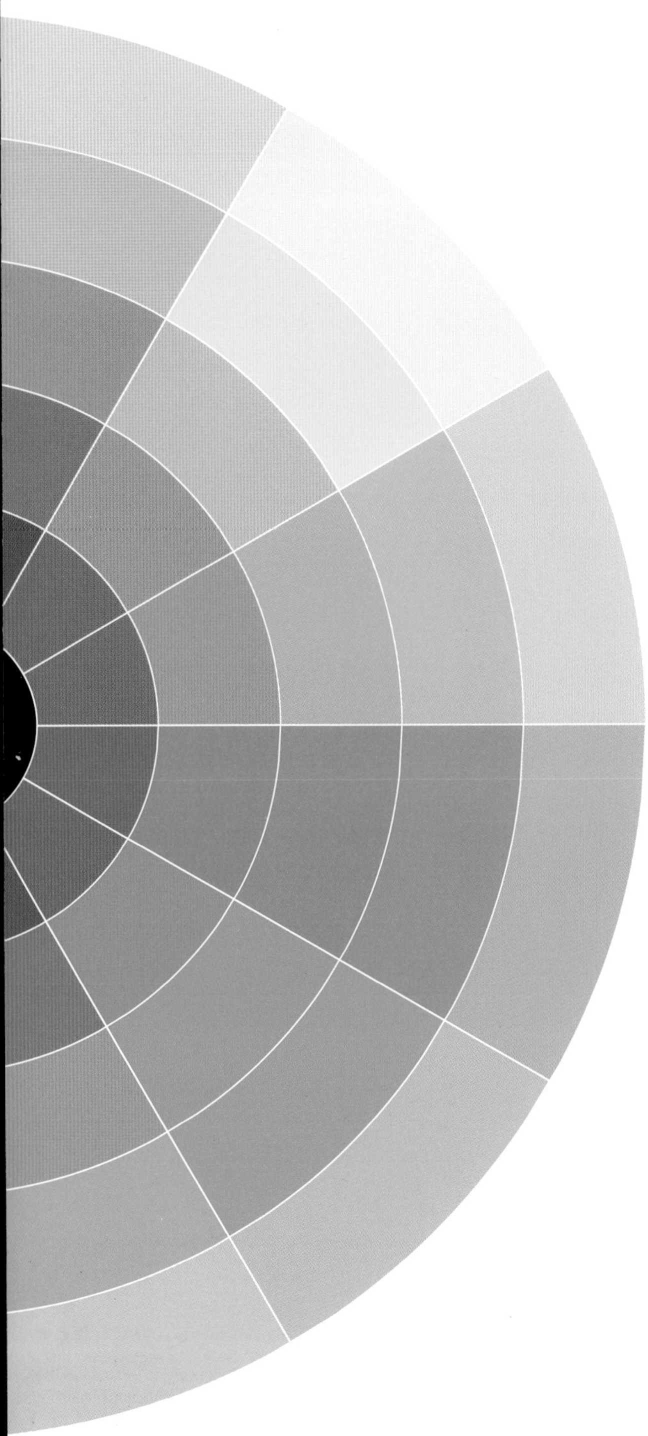

Below are some of my favourite colour combinations. All of them together might be too much, but for inspiration you could pick out two or three colours that appear next to each other in the list, such as purple, pink and black, or black, red and acid green.

I've put some Latin names in here, just so that if you want to ask for the plant, you can get exactly the right one.

Grey
Perovskia 'Blue Spire'
Hosta (Tardiana Group) 'Hadspen Blue'
Artemisia ludoviciana 'Silver Queen'

Purple
Salvia x *superba*
Allium sphaerocephalon
Cotinus coggygria 'Royal Purple'

Pink
Geranium psilostemon
Nerine bowdenii
Echinacea purpurea

Black
Phormium 'Platt's Black'
Ophiopogon planiscapus 'Nigrescens'
Tulipa 'Black Parrot'

Red
Rosa 'Geranium' (moyesii hybrid)
Tulipa 'Red Shine'
Hemerocallis 'Stafford'

Acid green
Euphorbia polychroma
Alchemilla mollis
Euphorbia schillingii

There's a website nursery specialising in black plants, called, appropriately enough, www.blackplants.co.uk

▲ Granite   ▲ York   ▲ Basalt   ▲ Slate   ▲ Limestone   ▲Granite and poured concrete   ▲Gravel

Floors

Choosing what to have on the floor of a garden is a really important and expensive decision. And it's not easy. Even if you do get hold of a few samples of materials, it's difficult to imagine what each will look like over a whole area. It is best to look out for a floor you like and then ask what it is made of. Ask not only what the material is but also how it was cut, how it was laid and what type of mortar there is in the joints.

For example, the material on the floor in this garden is granite. To get the same look you also need to know that it is:
● Sawn (so it has perfectly straight edges)
● Polished (so it almost shines)
● Butt jointed (so no mortar is in sight)
● Laid stretcher bond (rather than random or a more intricate and more old-fashioned-looking pattern)

15

facts about garden floors

James Weston of All Seasons Landscapes has been building gardens for over 10 years and has a degree in natural environmental science. That makes him the ideal person to give a few tips on choosing floor materials:

1   Natural products used to be much more expensive than manmade, but now you can get some really competitively priced natural stones, especially imported sandstones.

2   Yorkstone is a sandstone. So when people talk about imported York, they mean a sandstone that has been imported, usually from India.

3   Sandstone isn't necessarily sandy coloured – it comes in reds, greens and greys. Especially if you're buying imported sandstone, make sure you specify the colour.

4   If you want your paving to look pristine and sleek, ask for sawn and polished. If you want it to look rugged and aged, ask for it to be riven and tumbled.

▲ Concrete ▲ Brick ▲ Flint and slate ▲ York ▲ Slate ▲ York stone ▲ Porphyry

5 Something with a smooth finish will get more slippery when wet – so a sawn finish will be more slippery than a riven finish.

6 Always use special paving bricks – pavers – that are frost proof, rather than using building bricks.

7 Pavers are not the same as engineering bricks, which are shiny and industrial looking.

8 If you want to revamp your patio but are on a budget, you can lift the existing stones and relay them with brick lines, details or cobble insets to give them a new appearance.

9 For a more modern look, polished concrete is great but not easy to work with. But you can buy polished concrete tiles, so you get the look without all the trouble.

10 If you're laying paving it's worth taking the trouble to get the base right. You need a four-inch depth of well-consolidated hardcore. Dig the area out, put down the hardcore, hire a machine called a whacker plate that compacts the hardcore, and give the base a really good going over before you put down the paving.

11 Gravel is the cheapest way to hard landscape an area, cheap to buy and cheap to install.

12 There are lots of different kinds of gravel and it's worth going to a builder's merchant to look at the various types and sizes.

13 Very large gravel stones, especially if laid thickly, can be difficult to walk on; very small stones spread around the place. 10-millimetre stones are a good standard size. Keep to quite a thin layer for the best results.

14 Honey-coloured gravel looks classy and quite natural, white works well to get an unreal effect. And there are some really brazen colours if you want to go down that route.

15 One of my favourites, especially where there are children about, is self-binding gravel - there aren't any loose stones to be eaten, scattered or brought into the house. It's the sort of material that is used on the paths in stately homes or in French *boules* parks. It's got lots of fine material in the mixture, which when rolled beds down and binds together.

5

Country

DESIGN BRIEF
- **Create a family garden from a small, tapering area**
- **Terrace for outdoor eating**
- **Vegetable garden**
- **Low maintenance**

FEATURES
- **Decked 'woodland' seating area**
- **Wildlife pond**
- **Vegetable area**

This is one of those gardens that is a great advertisement for really good design. It's a completely awkward shape, tapering at one end to a point. It's pretty small, yet has to accommodate a family of five. At its widest point the ground is uneven, very damp in places and dominated by two huge yew trees. And to top it all, the family are away for weeks at a time so the garden has to be very low maintenance; in fact, it has to look after itself. Now that's a challenge.

But look at it now – it works. There's plenty for the children, the adults have what they wanted, the details in the garden are a joy and overall it looks stylish and inviting. The garden was created by its owners, garden designers James and Helen Dooley, and they have done a wonderful job turning a difficult area into a beautiful, functioning garden.

Hedges The garden is tiny, but hedges help to give structure to the space. Low hedges provide a subtle green division between the different areas.

Low brick wall To retain the view, there is a low brick wall on the boundary.

Planting The Dooleys use this border to experiment with different plant combinations and its content changes yearly.

Lawn Even in this small space there is room for a lawn. It keeps the area green and doesn't obstruct the view outwards.

Sandpit and vegetable area
A sandpit is tucked behind the yew hedge and beyond that is the vegetable area. This makes the most of the narrowest part of the garden. In a vegetable plot every square inch can be used, however narrow the area is.

Terrace The main seating area looks out to the open fields.

▲ **The walk-way** down to the pond has stepping stones in it – a lovely, simple idea to add to the fun.

▲ **An open fire** in a brazier is a stylish way to keep warm.

▲ **Even a tiny pond** like this attracts all sorts of wildlife and provides interest for the children.

▲ **Tucked away** in the corner of the vegetable area is a little sandpit.

▲ **The decked seating area** is surrounded by a screen of dogwood. The dogwood (Cornus) is used like willow, with live branches woven together to make a screen and stuck into the ground to take root. The planting around it nestles the deck into the surroundings. For the children it acts as a stage or a place to hide, and for the adults it's also a place to hide, with its candles and open fire.

▲ **Twigs** bent round to make different-sized circles and then bound together make a great target for arrows.

'This is apparently effortless good design, not showy and there's no huge statement, but providing a real working family garden. It is easy with itself and easy to live with, while still providing excitement and interest for the adults as well as the children.'

Design

In plan it's easy to see just what a challenge this garden was. But the area has been divided up into three spaces – each much more useable than the overall shape would lead you to believe possible. Even the narrowest point is used for growing vegetables.

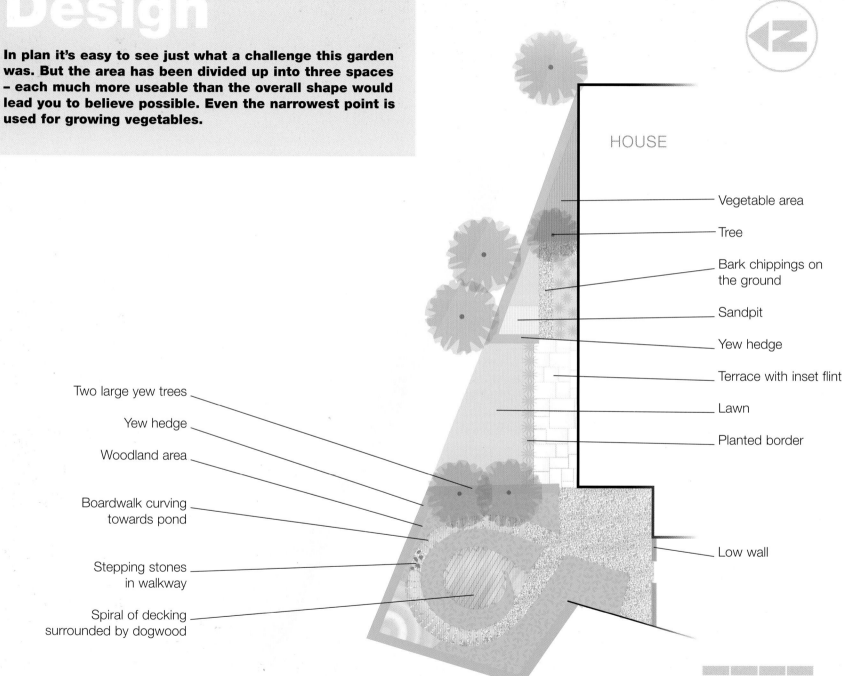

HOUSE

Vegetable area

Tree

Bark chippings on the ground

Sandpit

Yew hedge

Terrace with inset flint

Lawn

Planted border

Low wall

Two large yew trees

Yew hedge

Woodland area

Boardwalk curving towards pond

Stepping stones in walkway

Spiral of decking surrounded by dogwood

0 1 2 3 4 metres

1 It can be used to create changes of level for interest.

2 Decking can also make steps and overhangs quite easily.

3 Most designers go for treated wood rather than decking. It looks better and more natural. When I looked through the pictures for this book I realised not one of the gardens has purpose-made decking in it! A word of caution, though: plain treated wood gets even more slippery in the wet than grooved decking boards.

4 If you're creating a seating area, try to bed it into the garden. Plant around it. If the decking is in the corner of the garden, make a space between the deck and the fence behind for planting and plant around the front edge, only leaving a space or two to get into the area. Create an entrance.

8

tips to make decking work

What's wrong with decking?

Is decking really awful or has it just been overused? There may be truth in the thought that it's overused, but on the other hand decking can look terrible if it's just plonked in a garden without any thought.

5 Decking is great where the ground is uneven – it can flatten out a slope and create a useable area.

6 It also forms a space underneath, which is really useful for cables for speakers or for power. On roof gardens this is especially important – you can't dig down!

7 Board walks and decking paths, raised above the ground, can be really interesting and show what decking is all about.

8 You can paint decking to give a more modern look.

Gardening with children

6
tips for seeds

1 Look for the magic words 'direct sow' or 'sow outdoors', which mean the seeds can be put straight in the ground and there's no faffing around with seed trays and transplanting seedlings.

2 You can sow outdoors from May onwards and it's a really good idea to save a few seeds to sow in June and July. The later you sow, the later the flowers will come. As long as they have a chance to flower before the first frosts, this is a great way to get colour in the garden right through to September and October.

3 Sowing is really easy to do: just rough up the soil a little and let the kids scatter the seeds. The main thing is to try to make sure there aren't any really nasty weeds in the patch, like bindweed that will swamp the area before the seeds get going.

4 If the weather has been dry, it's worth giving the seeds a little water.

5 My favourite flower for kids is Cosmos. The foliage is lovely, the colours are great and the tall ones come up way above little children (in rich soil they will get to over 5 feet), so you can make a den for the children by planting the Cosmos in a circle.

6 Also try some smaller plants – again, you can get the kids to scatter the seeds about and they'll come up without any fuss – Nigella, Californian poppies, cornflowers.

6

ideas for quick and easy garden activities

1 **Match the leaf** Go around the garden and take a leaf off, say, five plants when the children aren't looking. Give the leaves to the children and ask them to find five exactly the same.

2 **Find the scent** Get the children to find three or five smelly plants and flowers in the garden.

3 **Make your initials in the lawn** Get the children to cut out their initials in cardboard and pin the cardboard down into the grass (or just weigh it down with stones). A week later the grass underneath will have become yellow – a great way to learn about chlorophyll.

4 **Daisy chains** Making daisy chains is an old idea but children still love doing it and it's a great excuse not to mow the lawn too often.

5 **Bug hunting** Ask the children to think about where the best place to find bugs would be and see how many different types of creatures they can find.

6 **Garden on a plate** Get the children to create a miniature garden on a plate. They can use twigs for trees, leaves for lawn, sticks for fences. You need to supply an old plate, but their imaginations should do the rest.

If you want more great ideas for children's projects, try Kim Wilde's book *Gardening with Children* (Collins, 2005).

Some dangerous plants to avoid

It's best to train your child not to eat plants in the garden – there are lots of poisonous plants and even more that will give them tummy ache if they eat enough of them. It's worth drumming into children not to eat anything unless an adult says it's OK.

Other plants can cause skin irritation, if children brush past them or pick a leaf and then touch their eyes they will be in a lot of pain. Euphorbia or spurge is the most common one. I do have it in my garden but in the front where the children don't play. Another is rue. Rue is a wonderful plant: evergreen, with a lovely shape to its leaves and will withstand a lot of neglect. However, it can cause really nasty skin blisters in some people.

Plants for children

Feeling – lambs' ears, soft grass.
Seeing – fuchsias: bright colours and it's great to pop the flower buds.
Also pansies, daisies and clematis all have great colours for children.
Hearing – bamboos of all kinds catch the wind and make music.
Scent – lavender, rosemary, thyme, mint.
Taste – strawberries, tomatoes, potatoes, courgettes.

(Photo C.Hockey)

(Photo C.Hockey)

▲ This sinuous fence screens off part of the garden but still has lots of gaps to see through and Carole has made sure that the gaps are just at the right level for children to use.

▲ This fence is in Carole's garden. The horizontals are brown (non-live) willow woven into a spiral. The uprights are living willow so they will sprout and grow above the fence below.

(Photo C.Hockey)

▲ A castle Carole built for children: the uprights have been left long to hang flags from.

▲ Using a metal top this willow den blends perfectly into the greenery behind. Made and photographed by Carole Hockey.

Making willow structures

Small willow structures are surprisingly easy to make and provide a natural play area or seating area for the garden. It's a great way to get children involved: not only can they design their own feature, they can also help to make it. Carole Hockey from Wildworks, who designs willow structures and supplies willow rods, points out that they're 'also good for wildlife, supporting insects and animals'.

Ingredients
Willow branches (called willow rods)
Implement to make planting holes for the rods – crowbar or strong metal stake
Ties to hold the weave together

How to get the rods
The Internet is the best source for rods generally.
The best willow is *Salix viminalis*, as its branches are straight and pliable.
For most structures you need one-year-old rods. If you're creating larger structures use two- or three-year-old rods for the uprights and one-year-old ones for the weave.
Once you've got one structure, the cuttings from that can supply you with additional rods for extensions.

When to create the structure
Willow rods are supplied during the winter and this is the best time to build the structure.

Where to build
Willow is amazingly versatile and will grow in pretty much any ground. It will do best, however, in full sun and reasonably good soil.

How to create a basic tunnel
- Plant uprights every 10 to 40 centimetres along the sides, using the metal stake to make the holes, which need to be about 30 centimetres deep.

- Between each upright plant two diagonal rods so they cross as near the ground as possible and will cross others further up the structure.

- To create the tunnel itself, tie together the uprights to form a series of archways.

- For additional strength weave in one-year-old rods along the sides and tie them in where necessary. These rods will eventually die, but by that time the new willow growth will have taken over their role.

Carole suggests that preparing the ground by clearing the weeds will give the willow the best start: 'Membrane does the trick but doesn't look very good – better just to weed around the base for the first year. After that they will be able to cope on their own.'

Maintenance
If it's dry in the first summer, water the structure occasionally. Each winter tie in shoots that can add to the structure and cut off any unwanted shoots.

Design
It's possible to make interlocking tunnels, windows, doorways, niches and domes, all using the same basic method. A tepee for little children is a great way to get started.

'Everyone likes this fresh green space that's enclosed by willow, it feels lovely to be sitting amongst the trees.'

Silver, Green & White

DESIGN BRIEF
- **Create three rooms**
- **Minimalist**
- **Limited colour palette**

FEATURES
- **White wall**
- **Rill running into lawn**
- **Limestone paving**

This garden may be minimal, but it's not plain and it's certainly not boring. This rectangular rear area has been transformed into a wonderfully stylish garden. The layout is quite straightforward: it's divided into three areas. The owner wanted to create 'three additional rooms: a dining room, a garden and a hideaway'.

Together they form a brilliant and beautifully proportioned garden, all the more amazing as it was laid out by the owner, who has no formal design training. He knew the look he wanted before he started: he explains, 'I wanted something minimalist but also green.' What he's achieved here is a deceptively simple design, but one that works hard and looks striking.

'When we created the garden we wanted to make extra rooms for the house, so we divided it into three separate areas. We wanted them to be the best rooms in the house; and they are.'

Walls The boundary walls are covered with thick ivy. This is a wonderful way to create consistency and give greenery to the boundaries, but the walls need to be maintained vigorously to keep the ivy looking neat.

Colours The garden has a very limited palette. Green, white and black are the main colours, with highlights of silver in the decorations and containers.

Box balls The garden only has three different types of permanent planting (ivy, box and bamboo at the back). Not only does this limited planting palette look good, it also makes the maintenance much simpler. These box balls are lined up along each side of the garden, providing a simple evergreen repeated pattern.

Containers Two topiaried Japanese hollies stand at either side of the entrance to the main garden and give height and structure. Further back, two tree ferns in silver containers mark the rear corners.

Cross wall Towards the rear of the garden stands a white wall with a dark slit exactly in its centre. The wall is great fun for the children – and the adults – creating as it does a hidden area behind. The wall also acts as a screen for playing movies on at night and is a great backdrop for fireworks.

Water feature At the base of the slit in the wall is a narrow channel of water, so narrow that it's safe for children (they can't get their faces in it).

▲ **Modern** silver-coloured containers with tree ferns mark the entrance to the seating area behind the wall.

▲ **Close to the house** the first area is a dining room with a seating area and shade from the sun.

▲ **To reinforce** the clean white lines of the garden a small wall, which has been rendered and painted, runs all the way around the sides.

▲ **Behind the wall** is a completely secluded seating area surrounded by bamboos. With a built-in seat and power, it's a place to relax, plug in the i-Pod and escape.

▲ **Perfect symmetry** The slit in the wall marks the central line of symmetry; without it the wall would be too stark, too austere. And the proportions are perfect: the wall is just the right height to hold the area without overpowering it.

The slit is very clever, painted black to stand out and mark the central line of the garden. It is wider at the front than the rear, so you can see out when you're behind it, but can't see in from the front.

'This garden is the perfect fusion of adults' and children's needs. The children, even in winter, can run around, play outside and hide behind the wall. They can put their hands in the running water but be quite safe. For the adults they have a beautiful space to enjoy and for eating out, for entertaining and for watching movies.'

Design

The beautiful, symmetrical simplicity of this garden can be seen from the plan. There are two quite different ways of dividing the garden. Between the deck and the garden there is a low wall with a central entrance. Between the garden and the rear sitting area is a central wall with entrances either side. Neither division is at all total but between them they create absolute seclusion for the rear sitting area.

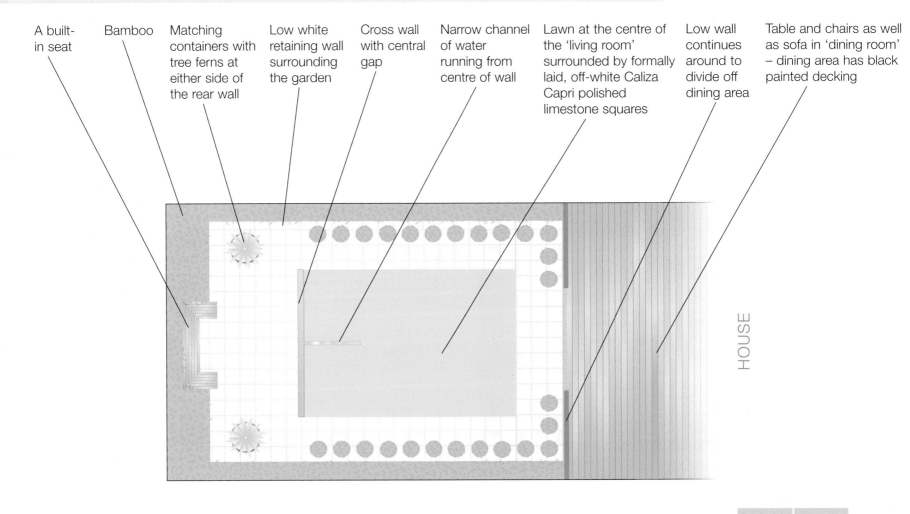

A built-in seat

Bamboo

Matching containers with tree ferns at either side of the rear wall

Low white retaining wall surrounding the garden

Cross wall with central gap

Narrow channel of water running from centre of wall

Lawn at the centre of the 'living room' surrounded by formally laid, off-white Caliza Capri polished limestone squares

Low wall continues around to divide off dining area

Table and chairs as well as sofa in 'dining room' – dining area has black painted decking

HOUSE

0   1   2 metres

Dividing the garden

What?
A garden can be divided into different areas, just as a house is divided into rooms.

Places to visit
The two gardens often most associated with garden rooms are Hidcote Manor Garden in Gloucestershire and Sissinghurst Castle Garden in Kent. Both are run by the National Trust (www.nationaltrust.org.uk).

In addition, if you go to almost any great garden, from the Alhambra in Spain, to Villa Lante in Italy, to Parc André Citroën in Paris, you'll see that they are divided into different rooms, each with a different character.

How?
The ways of creating divisions are fairly easy to reel off: shrubs and trees, trellis and, as in this garden, walls. The divisions don't have to be total; they can be implied. The wall here between the dining area and the play area is very low, but along with different floor materials, it creates a feeling of two separate rooms.

Where?
Where to put the divisions and how high should they be? This is where the artistry begins. It comes down to proportions, to creating useful spaces that are a joy to be in. There are several suggestions to help you to achieve the right proportions:

- You can go by eye. This is often the best way, as garden design is an inexact science and what you're trying to achieve is just something that looks right.
- You can use the proportions of the house as a guide.
- You can go for straightforward halves or thirds.

But a great tip is, however you do it, mark out the areas on the ground with paint before you start and live with them for a while. Walk through the areas to make sure they feel right.

Why?
- To make the spaces in the garden have more pleasing proportions (and to escape from really nasty proportions). One of the most common reasons for wanting to divide the garden up is when you're dealing with a very long and thin garden. The space feels wrong. Divide it up into rooms that are only slightly longer than they're wide and you begin to enjoy the space.
- To make the space seem bigger. Even the smallest gardens will appear to be larger if they are divided up and given some hidden areas. The rooms also tend to hide the boundaries – if you can't see how small a garden is, you can imagine it being a lot larger.
- To create interest, mystery and surprise. In this garden there's a surprise behind the wall: the seating area. Another benefit of forming rooms is to create a journey around the garden. In a very small garden it might be pushing it to call it a 'journey', but perhaps a jaunt from one area to the next is possible.
- To hide things and for people to hide. Especially in cities, having somewhere secluded and away from it all is incredibly important. If all of your garden is on view there won't be anywhere for you to hide.
- Framing the view. Division does tend to create frames. In this garden there's a view back, through the slit, and again this adds to the interest.
- For fun. All that interest and mystery and hiding are great fun, especially for children. In this garden the kids can run round and round the wall, peer out and create hidden dens.

1

3

4

Instant gardening:
Containers

Containers are a great way to do instant gardening. You get structure and greenery in a flash. They're enjoyably fickle as well – move the planters round (if they're not too big) to create new scenes and change what's in them to suit your mood or the season.

2

5

6

1. **Big**   There aren't many containers in this garden, but they have a lot of impact. Two cloud-pruned hollies stand at the entrance to the main garden and two tree ferns are placed at the rear entrances to the secluded area.
2. **Traditional**   This container of Cannas and grass is a traditional summer choice.
3. **Traditional with a twist**   A traditional container, but not a traditional plant – this is lawn grass.
4. **Stylish**   Traditional terracotta pots placed either side of the entrance with wonderful hydrangeas about to flower. In the winter the hydrangeas will just be sticks, but they can be moved out of the way and replaced by a winter-performing pair of plants.
5. **Splash of colour**   Geraniums are very traditional summer bedding plants, but choose an outrageously bright colour and put them in a line of pots and they become a stylish statement.
6. **Classy**   Simple shapes of box in plain containers are stylish and will last all year round.

What doesn't work?

People often talk about 'plants suitable for containers', but really you can grow anything in a container. Some plants outgrow their containers quite quickly; expect only to get a few years out of a tree in a container, for example. Very thirsty plants will need a lot of attention. Leggy and formless plants don't look very good in containers.

But I'd try anything, as long as it looks good. Here's a quick guide to proportions in containers.

▲ This garden was created by Foxes Boxes who can do the whole design for window boxes and balconies as well as providing colourful containers.

◀ This shows what a stunning display of containers can achieve. These geometric pots from Capital Garden Products have been arranged to make a statement.

Copper ▶ planters from Privett are wonderful for a modern, sleek look.

◀ Urns like this can look good as a statement, on either side of an entrance, or just hidden amongst the foliage. This one is from Capital Garden Products.

If you want to ▶ really make a statement with your containers try these enormous and colourful ones from Privett.

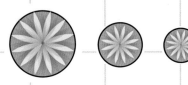

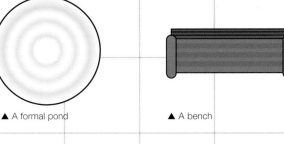

▲ Potted Plants

▲ A formal pond

▲ A bench

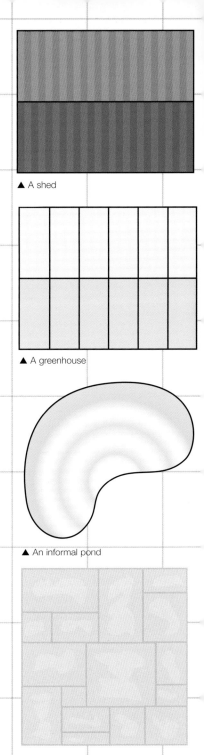

▲ A shed

▲ A greenhouse

▲ An informal pond

▲ Paving

tips for designing your own garden

The two most common things people say when they try to design their own garden are 'I just don't know where to start' and the opposite, 'I've got so many ideas, I want to include them all!' It's difficult to know how to begin but there is a logical way to design a garden that works. Here's a brief outline.

A book on garden design

If you want to tackle the design of your own garden, try reading *A Handbook for Garden Designers* by Rosemary Alexander and Karena Batstone (Cassell, 2005). It's the book that garden designers use.

1 **Draw** Do a scale drawing. Measure up the garden and draw it out, to scale, on paper. For a small to medium garden, 2 centimetres for each metre will usually do. Mark on the drawing anything that is going to impinge on the design: a tree you can't remove, a view you want to hide, entrances and exits. Don't put anything on the drawing that you don't want to keep. You can see immediately that, in many ways, a smaller garden is easier to tackle yourself.

2 **The look** It's best to have a clear idea of the look of the garden before you start. This helps to narrow down the possibilities. The owner here took inspiration from the Hempel Hotel in London, which has a lawn defined by light-coloured paving with contemporary planting around it. If you can find inspiration from a single photograph or garden, the design will come more easily and be more uniform.

3 **Uses** Consider how you want to use the garden; this too will narrow down how you divide up the space. Here the owner knew he wanted three areas and the design flowed from there.

4 **Leave** It's best not to sit in the garden or look at it when you're designing a new one. It's too easy to be distracted by what's there now. Go inside with the scale drawing and your inspiration.

5 **Contractors** Unless you're very keen at do-it-yourself, once you've got the outline of your design it's probably worth calling on contractors to build the garden. Good contractors will not just implement the plan but will improve on it.

6 **Help** If you do get stuck, a professional garden designer can help enormously. Even if you want to do the design yourself, many garden designers will come along for a one-off consultation to talk through any problems you're having or to set you off in the right direction. Most garden designers have websites so you can see if their style fits with your ideas.

Use this grid to help you do a scale drawing of your garden - for each metre of your garden use one square of the grid (2cm). The symbols on the opposite page might help as well

0   0.5   1 metres

Water, Light & Walls

DESIGN BRIEF
- **A garden for the family**
- **A sensory garden**
- **To complement the house**

FEATURES
- **Child-safe fishpond**
- **No lawn**
- **Perspex panels in walls**

If there's one garden that sums up what this book is all about, it's this one.

Out went the lawn, out went the play frame, out went the dull little borders. In their place are structural walls, exciting planting, water and light. And do you know what? The children play in this garden much, much more than in the old, traditional one. Paul Dracott, from Agave Garden Design, has created a garden that works for both adults and children.

'Before we started the garden was a typical 1950s area with a garage at the back and a central lawn. There was a play frame but the children rarely used it, but now they are always out there.'

Walls Light-coloured walls with sure, clean lines divide up the garden into separate 'rooms'. The walls look stunning and create lots of areas for the children to discover, play and hide in.

Safe fishpond There's a fishpond under the walkway, protected by a metal grid, so it's safe for children but they can watch the fish beneath.

Planting The planting is billowy and abundant to contrast with the stark lines of the walls. It is made up of large areas of just a few plants. These are plants that grow and flower during the summer, die off but keep standing through winter, and are then cut down in early spring.

Flooring Different materials on the floor help to reinforce the different rooms.

Silhouettes Frosted Perspex partitions allow the plants to create shadows, seen from the other side as silhouettes. And there are coloured lights, for the children to create shadows and silhouettes too.

No lawn There is no grass in the garden, so the area needs to be divided up quite strongly or it would become a mass of planting and paths.

▲ **After dark,** water and light provide extra excitement to the garden.

▲ **Busy and bright** planting is used on the warm, south-facing terrace next to the house.

▲ **The seating area** at the rear of the garden is a perfectly proportioned room.

▲ **Black-eyed Susan** and Miscanthus form blocks of planting. The black-eyed Susan comes to life in early autumn, while the Miscanthus grass develops through the summer and by autumn is tall and golden.

Around the seating area have been placed quite mature silver birch trees, for both their light canopy and their lovely white trunks.

'This garden looks wonderful and has so much to interest children and stimulate their senses. This sums up the fusion of needs that go to create a true family garden: children don't have to be shunted off to a corner of the garden and the garden doesn't have to be compromised by their needs. In garden design, as elsewhere, both children and adults respond to exciting design and stimulating spaces.'

Design

For a garden of this size to work without a lawn the structure has to be immaculate. The walls give the main structure, backed up by changes in floor material and strong planting in the beds.

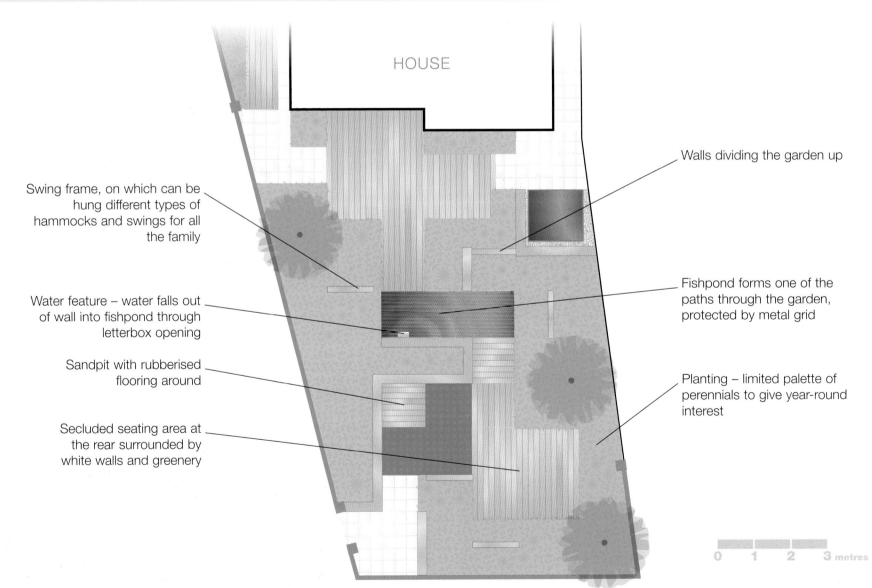

HOUSE

Swing frame, on which can be hung different types of hammocks and swings for all the family

Water feature – water falls out of wall into fishpond through letterbox opening

Sandpit with rubberised flooring around

Secluded seating area at the rear surrounded by white walls and greenery

Walls dividing the garden up

Fishpond forms one of the paths through the garden, protected by metal grid

Planting – limited palette of perennials to give year-round interest

0   1   2   3 metres

The outside room

Popularising the idea of using the garden as an outside room is attributed to John Brookes, one of the greats of modern British garden design. This concept takes the garden away from being a place just to practise gardening to being a place, like any other room, to be enjoyed and decorated.

Once you treat the garden as an additional room (or rooms) to the house, several factors follow:

Seating areas become more important as outdoor eating in an outside dining room becomes popular. So we see the rise of patios.

Decorations are needed in the garden for us to enjoy as we sit on our patios. So there's been a huge rise in the popularity of water features, sculptures and containers.

We like to redecorate our outside room with instant plants and painted fences, just as we would redecorate a room inside the house. It's amazing to think that not that long ago (before garden centres) plants had to be ordered and waited for, and were often only available at certain times of the year.

Children want to play in these rooms where before they would be kept out of the garden so they didn't spoil the plants.

In fact, pretty much everything in this or any other modern garden book comes from this idea of using the garden in different ways but as an integral part of the living space. Sometimes it's even used for gardening......

John Brookes also came up with a sound idea for helping to design such a garden. He suggests using some proportions from the house to divide the garden up. It is a fairly simple and pretty foolproof way to get a ground-plan design that works with the scale of the house, so that, as John says, 'proportionally they tie together to create a room outside'.

Using the same proportions imposes a unity between house and garden and ensures the garden rooms are an easy size to live with.

The idea is incredibly simple in essence: take a major measurement from the house, in the case of this garden the rear double doors (1.2 metres wide), and use this measurement, or multiples of it, when dividing up the garden. As Paul Dracott says, 'This relates the garden to the house and creates a garden with restful, ordered proportions.' And using the house as a guideline for the garden means that the 'two work together, flow easily and the garden doesn't look just stuck on'.

Even beyond the exact measurements you might use, this idea gets you thinking on the right lines: that designing a garden is about making spaces. These spaces are to be used and need to link together.

Often when people are designing their garden they get bogged down by trying to work with the garden's overall shape. It's a bit like building a house on a plot of land: you don't build the house to fit exactly into the shape of the plot, you build the house to try to use the space, but what is most important is that the house and its rooms feel and look right.

John Brookes has written many books on garden design: probably the best known is called, appropriately enough, *John Brookes Garden Design* (Dorling Kindersley, 2001).

New perennial planting

One of the latest trends to really catch on in planting is the use of perennials (plants that live for several years but tend to die back over winter, to re-emerge the following spring).

Traditional herbaceous borders also use a lot of perennial planting, so how is this different?
The difference is in which plants are used and how they're used (see table).

And if anyone says, 'Oh that's lovely but it won't work in a small garden,' look at the garden in this chapter.

HERBACEOUS BORDER PLANTING	NEW PERENNIAL PLANTING
Plants from all sorts of different habitats with different needs put together	Plants chosen to suit the environment of the garden
Small numbers of a wide range of plants	Large numbers of a narrow range of plants
Planted in threes and fives	Planted in large drifts
Regimented layers according to size, with tallest at back	Arranged drifts, sometimes with taller plants towards front
Staking required	Plants chosen to stand up by themselves
Dividing required	Plants chosen so they work together without one of them becoming dominant – so they create a stable community
Cut down at end of October	Leave over winter – plants chosen that will 'die well' and carry on looking good through the winter, which is also good for wildlife
Intensive maintenance	If planned well these borders can be very low maintenance

Books on the new perennial planting
Two names associated with this type of planting are Piet Oudolf and Noel Kingsbury. *Designing with Plants* (Piet Oudolf with Noel Kingsbury, Conran Octopus, 1999) is a lovely book and *The New Perennial Garden* (Noel Kingsbury, Frances Lincoln, 2001) is inspirational.

▲ Miscanthus sinensis

▲ Rudbeckia fulgida

▲ Phlomis tuberosa

▲ Echinacea pupurea 'Green Edge'

▲ Echinops ritro 'Veitch's Blue'

10 plants for perennial planting

The list of plants you could try is enormous, but here are a few of the best 'doers' for sunny beds in average soil. These should provide interest right through to autumn and winter, to be cut back in early spring. Apologies for the Latin names, but it pays to be very specific about which plants you need.

▲ Verbena bonariensis

▲ Sanguisorba 'Tanna'

▲ Persicaria amplexicaulis 'Rosea'

▲ Sedum telephium 'Matrona'

▲ Astrantia major

Lighting

Lighting is an exciting and upcoming area of garden design. Paul Dracott has noticed a distinct change: 'More often now people are asking for lighting, ten years ago no one did.' Why? 'People like to eat outside now but also there's a fashion in interior design to have no window dressing so you look out to the garden from the house more. People are also realising that lighting can create a wonderful view, especially in the winter.'

▲ These have spikes to put in the ground – a great outdoor way to use tealights (from The Urban Garden).

8

lighting tips from Paul Dracott

1 Think about what will be in the garden in winter and what can be used for lighting effects.

2 Light the background plants in white for structure and then highlight with coloured lights.

3 Don't use too many different colours, three at most.

4 Blue works really well to highlight both steelwork and water.

5 From the main viewpoint of the garden you shouldn't see the light source. It's the effects of the lights you want to see, not the bright source.

6 Light the foreground and the background but keep the midground dark: if there's too much lighting the picture begins to look one-dimensional.

7 Even if you aren't putting lighting in, when you do your garden put the cables down so that there's provision to add it later.

8 There are different ways to use light, for example:

Uplighting – putting lights under trees and structures. This is particularly effective in the winter.

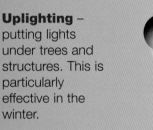

Moonlighting – lights that shine onto the ground of the garden.

Shadowing – shining light through strong forms and projecting onto flat surfaces.

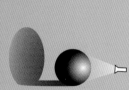

Grazing – shining light along the surface of a wall to bring out its texture.

◀ From Cox & Cox this lovely glass storm lantern with etched stars is just right to hang from a tree.

Candle holders ▶ from Ambient Home look great in the garden, they come in pairs and are substantial enough to keep out the breeze.

◀ These gas flared torches come from The Urban Garden and have their own gas supply so you just turn it on, light the gas and bingo, there's light.

A lovely lantern ▶ to hang from a branch or put on a wall, from The Urban Garden

8

Height & Depth

DESIGN BRIEF
- **Low maintenance**
- **Encourage the children into the garden**
- **Flowers**

FEATURES
- **Purpose-built climbing frame**
- **Steps lit from behind**
- **Rendered but unpainted walls**

This garden is typical of many small city backyards. Below ground level, it's reached by steep steps going down from the ground floor of the house. This sort of deep-set garden can be very forbidding and, if you've got one that's been neglected, it's difficult to see how it could ever become a place you would want to spend time in.

That's the situation that faced Claire Mee, the designer, when she first saw the deep well of a garden on this site.

'It was such a waste, neither the children nor the adults wanted to go outside. A central part of the brief was to encourage the four children out of the house.'

Built-in seating
This helps to reinforce the structure of the garden, it saves on space and there's storage underneath. It also looks a lot neater and you don't have to drag seats in and out of storage through the year.

Paving A hard surface means that the children can ride bicycles around all through the year.

Low wall This low wall partitions the garden into rooms without cutting off parts of the space.

Safer steps The steps down have been made wider and safer for the children with a sturdy handrail.

Vertical planting In a tiny, sunken garden like this the walls are incredibly dominant. Instead of looking on them as a problem, they've been treated here as an opportunity for more planting, with climbers and trees filling the beds.

▲ **The Perspex screens** of the risers have lights behind them.

▲ **Raised beds** also help to decrease the dominance of the walls. The visible wall starts at 50 centimetres up from the ground.

▲ **The climbing frame** is tall and tucked into the corner of the garden. It makes the most of the depth of the garden.

▲ **Cordoned apple** trees cover the walls and provide fruit from the garden for the children.

▲ **Built-in seating** in a cosy corner has been made possible by the low dividing wall. The seating also provides storage for garden equipment. The wall behind has been rendered but not painted.

'This garden, while small, has a lot of potential in its height. The boundary walls provide extra growing room and also create proportions that allow tall structures and plants. Claire has made the most of this dimension in her design. The play frame is tall and thin and if the garden wasn't surrounded by walls this would look out of place, but nestled against the house it blends into the dimensions of the area. Similarly Claire has taken the opportunity to use taller trees that can grow up, use the height and soften the boundaries. If those boundaries weren't there the trees would look out of place. Within the harsh confines of the area Claire has brought in a soft yet structured garden that meets both the needs of children and adults.'

Design

Seen from above the climbing frame is incredibly unobtrusive and the main part of the garden is formed from a beautiful sitting area and raised beds.

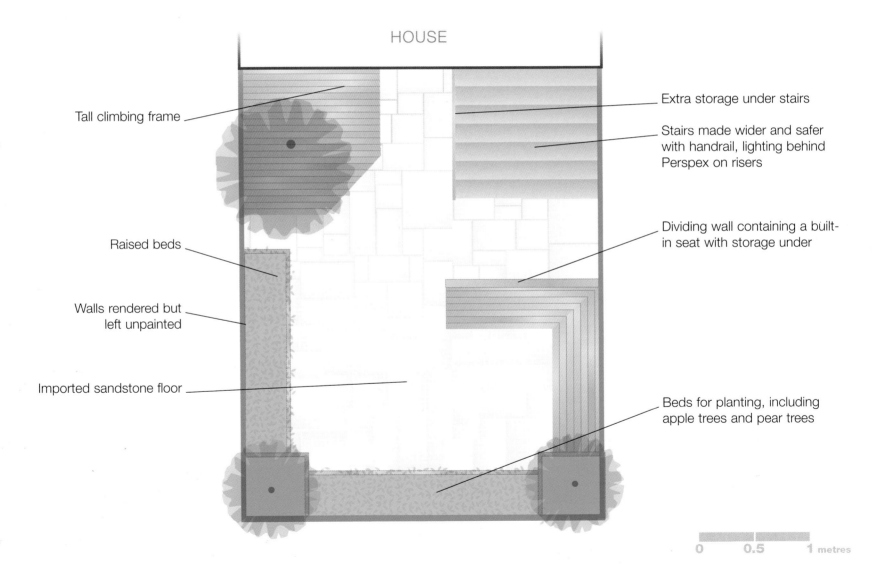

HOUSE

Tall climbing frame

Raised beds

Walls rendered but left unpainted

Imported sandstone floor

Extra storage under stairs

Stairs made wider and safer with handrail, lighting behind Perspex on risers

Dividing wall containing a built-in seat with storage under

Beds for planting, including apple trees and pear trees

0   0.5   1 metres

Growing food

Food from the garden is a wonderful thing – it's healthy, can be educational for children, and it tastes better. But if you're busy with a family and if your garden is small, growing food is probably way down your list of priorities.

I used to have an allotment and a greenhouse; now I've got a family. I still have three strawberry plants, half a dozen lettuces and a courgette. Where before I grew many things from seeds, I bought these from the local garden centre as young plants. But it's something, and my children can watch and wait for the strawberries to ripen, they can pick the courgettes and then eat them for tea. What I'm saying is that unless you're going for self-sufficiency, it isn't quantity that's important.

So start small. If the plants don't die and you do enjoy the produce, next year do a little more. The worst thing, if you're not a keen gardener, is to make a huge patch of vegetables and feel like you have to fill it. It will just be a chore rather than a pleasure.

A great book that lays out all the information you need to start with vegetables is *The Vegetable and Herb Expert* by D.G. Hessayon (Expert Books, 1997).

5 tips for starting out on growing food

1 Unless you really want to spend time on gardening, don't create a large vegetable and fruit area. A hole in the planting or a container will do; treat them as you would annual bedding.
2 At first buy small plants rather than grow vegetables or fruit from seed. It's not the most economic way to grow food, but it's less work and you're more likely to succeed.
3 Put the plants somewhere that gets some sun, is near the house (so you don't forget about them completely) and can be watered easily.
4 Strawberries are my number one plant for non-gardeners. They don't need work, the flowers are pretty and the produce is very popular. I like to grow lettuces too, as you can be sure yours haven't been sprayed or treated. You can also buy different colours of lettuces that look quite pretty together.
5 Sweetcorn is great to watch as it grows so high, although whether your plant produces anything or not is dependent on the summer weather.

5 tips if you decide to be earnest about edibles

1 A separate area means you can keep an eye on everything at once and specially created beds will help to organise the area. But a vegetable patch can also be pretty; when it's pretty it's called a potager. A potager can have seats, fountains and ornamental plants, like box or thyme, around the edges that keep it looking good all year round.
2 Creating raised beds means you can monitor the quality of the soil that goes into them and make sure it doesn't have too many weeds in it.
3 Paths should be just over a metre wide if you want to get a wheelbarrow down them. A good size for beds is just over a metre square so you can reach in without standing on the soil.
4 Traditionally plants have been put in dead straight rows, so you know exactly where your vegetables are and you can weed between them more easily.
5 It is good to give children an area of the vegetable patch where they can grow their own plants. At first expect to do most of the work yourself, but it'll still be their carrots they eat for tea and their pumpkins they make into lanterns at Halloween.

▲ Wisteria

▲ Honeysuckle

▲ Clematis

Vertical planting

Rather than seeing tall walls as a problem, look on them as an opportunity for extra planting space. Climbers are the first choice for this.

Climbing plants

Most climbers will need support, either wires or trellis to grow up. And in many ways this is good: you can decide where they will grow and they won't impinge on the wall itself.

If you go for self-clingers, like ivy or Virginia creeper, you don't need to provide support, but they do have a tendency to run away and will damage loose render or pointing.

Climbers for a small space (these all need support)

Clematis   Different varieties flower right through the year even in the middle of winter.

Wisteria   Deciduous, with delicate leaves and either purple or white flowers; the stems are quite beautiful even in winter.

Passionflower   A semi-evergreen that is not entirely hardy but will do fine on a sheltered wall, especially in a town or city. The flowers are wonderful and it romps away to cover walls, and entire houses if you let it!

Honeysuckle   Scented summer flowers in white, yellow or orange.

Ornamental vine   Don't try to eat the grapes, they're sour, but the plant is lovely with a touch of the Mediterranean to it. The leaves don't stay through the winter.

▲ Ornamental vine
▼ Passionflower

▲ Snowy mespilus
▼ Cordoned pear

▲ Step over espaliered apple.

Trees

Trees can also be used against walls and espaliered (fan-trained) fruit trees are ideal for this. In this garden two pears have been used, *Pyrus communis* 'Beurré Hardy', *Pyrus communis* 'Doyenné du Comice', and one apple tree, *Malus* 'Canada Grey Queen'. These will provide blossom in spring and fruit in the autumn. One caveat: fruit trees need pollinating in order to set fruit. It's a complicated business to get the right trees together, so it's worth buying from a good nursery and taking their staff's advice on which ones you need.

Play equipment

This garden's solution of a purpose-built climbing area is brilliant. It uses the depth of the area while having a small footprint on the ground so it doesn't take up the whole garden. The climbing frame is built around an existing tree, which gives added interest and helps to make it feel part of the garden. Because the frame was built for the site, the clients were able to specify exactly what they (and their children) wanted. Claire Mee says, 'It's really not difficult to make your own climbing equipment or have it made for you and you'll get something that fits the site and your needs perfectly. In this case, it had to work around the tree so we had to get it made specially.'

There's a hidden den area at the base and various ways to climb to a higher platform. With four offspring and their friends using the frame, the play equipment had to accommodate lots of children and a climbing frame can do this with minimum bickering.

This is a really neat sandpit for a smaller garden from Urchin, with a lid to keep the rain out!

A great idea ▶ from Letterbox to make climbing a bit easier for little ones - a rope ladder with three sides.

If there are fewer children or your children are good at sharing, swings are good. But you need quite a lot of space to swing properly and you need lots of room around to make sure children aren't going to walk into the swing's path all the time.

A variation on a swing, I've found that a huge hammock is a wonderful piece of play equipment for children. They can pretend it's a pirate ship or just lie and swing – and of course it's good for adults too.

A frame for different types of swinging things is a great solution to get the most out of the space in a small garden. Everything from a baby swing to a swinging seat for an adult can be hooked on this frame.

◀ It's fun, it's tough and it's made from recycled materials. This tyre horse swing from Urchin is great for younger children.

Just right for ▶ adults to lie on but also great fun for children, this free-standing hammock is from Cox & Cox.

Exotic Heat Island

DESIGN BRIEF
- **Interesting plants**
- **Play areas for children**
- **Lawn**

FEATURES
- **Den for children**
- **Raised beds**
- **Bicycle shelter**

A new extension was the impetus for changing the garden here. The brief was for a garden that the two boys (aged 6 and 9) could play in, but also one in which the adults could 'indulge their love of plants'.

However, straight away there was a huge problem. There is concrete nearly a metre thick on the ground and it couldn't be removed, so there was no soil for the lawn to establish itself and no soil for plants.

The landscape architect on the project, Karen Fitzsimon, came up with an ingenious solution: she's used roof garden technology and know-how to create a garden here. On the ground is Geovoid 30 by Greenfix, which is a water-dispensing material that basically acts like soil but achieves the results in millimetres rather than metres. It holds sufficient water for the grass but doesn't get waterlogged. And for the plants there are raised beds to create a good depth of soil.

Planting The planting is in raised beds so that the plants can have a good depth of soil. This solution has other benefits: many of the plants are delicate and they can be appreciated better in their raised position, and the raised beds also help to keep the children, and their footballs, off the plants.

Pond A pond has been included; it's tiny but still big enough to grow aquatic plants and attract some wildlife.

Lawn The lawn is growing on hardly any depth of soil. Just below it is deep concrete, but the high-tech membrane (usually used on roof gardens) allows the lawn to grow happily with just enough water.

Hideaway In the corner a secret hideaway acts as a den for children and a study for adults.

▲ **Looking from the front** of the house down what was a passageway.

▲ **The pond** contains aquatic plants and has a step up for any frogs that come to visit.

▲ **Even the bicycle** shed is beautifully thought out. Made by the English Garden Carpentry Company.

▲ **Seen from the below-ground** kitchen, the garden takes on another dimension. The raised beds, a necessity because of the lack of soil, have been turned into an advantage, giving the garden a wonderful structure and plenty of impromptu seating.

▲ **In the corner of the garden** is the hideaway. It's an exciting place for the children but will, as Karen says, 'hold its own in the garden as a feature once the kids have moved on from it'.

'This was a tricky garden to design, with many demands being put on a very small space and there was of course the huge drawback of the lack of soil. But rather than go for the easy route, Karen and the owners have taken the time to make a unique garden, with detailing and features that could so easily have been left out, but would have been missed. The garden has an organic, bespoke feel, which along with the exotic planting make this a very personal creation.'

Design

There's a rule in garden design – keep it simple – and this garden does just that. But the simple layout belies the clever responses to the challenges the space threw at the designer and client.

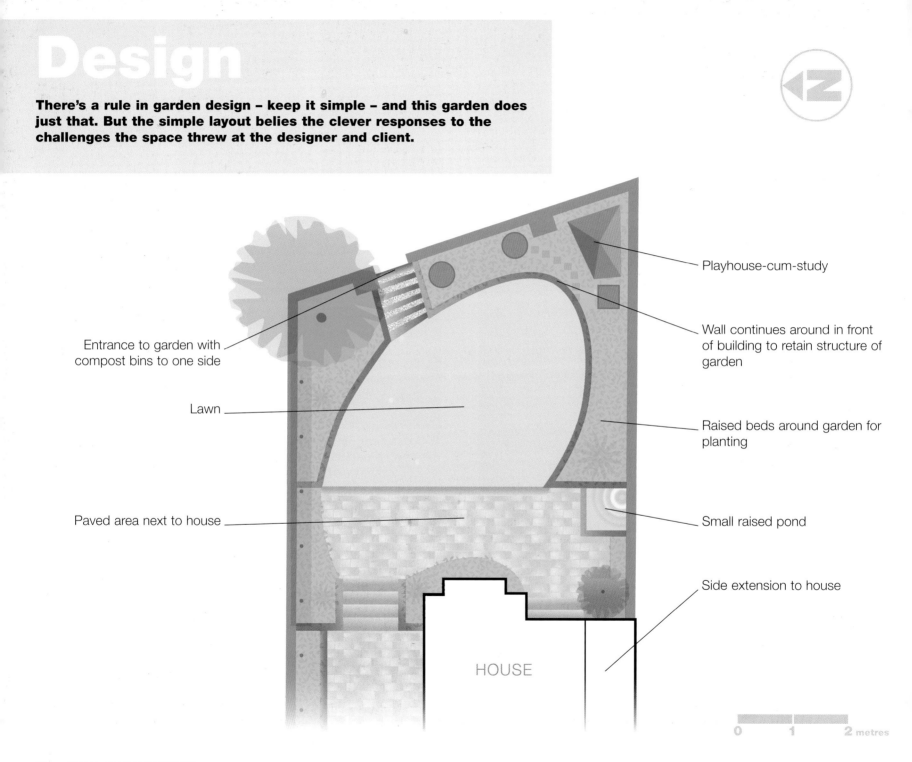

Entrance to garden with compost bins to one side

Lawn

Paved area next to house

Playhouse-cum-study

Wall continues around in front of building to retain structure of garden

Raised beds around garden for planting

Small raised pond

Side extension to house

HOUSE

0   1   2 metres

Creating a small wildlife pond

Even the smallest pond will attract pond skaters, damselflies and dragonflies. In spring there will probably be frogspawn and later frogs and toads to watch out for. Around the pond greenery will allow small animals to hide safely and a sloping edge can be useful for both children and animals. A slope is safer for children as they aren't confronted with a steep drop and if it's covered with sand or pebbles it makes a great 'beach'. The slope will also help animals get out of the water if they fall in accidentally.

Suppliers of native plants for ponds
Try Honeysome Aquatics, The Row, Sutton, Nr Ely, Cambridgeshire CB6 2PB Tel. 01353 778889

6 tips for wildlife ponds

1 **Siting the pond** In a small garden you may not have a lot of choice about where to put a pond. But if you do have a choice, consider the following aspects:
• Try to avoid putting a pond under a tree because the falling leaves can pollute the water.
• If you need power for a pump or filter you need to make the pond near a power source.
• With a pond for wildlife one of the great things, especially for children, is to be able to sit close and watch the goings-on, so put a bench or seat nearby.

2 **Size** The bigger the better. In bigger ponds you can grow a greater diversity of plants, which helps the pond look after itself.

3 **Materials** For small ponds a pre-formed rigid liner might be best, for larger ponds flexible UPVC tends to be a better option. Whichever you go for, don't skimp on quality as there are a lot of strains on the liners and sunlight will tend to add to the wear and tear.

4 **Sides** Make sure the sides aren't too steep for frogs. Also a rockery or lots of damp vegetation will provide shelter for amphibians.

5 **Plants** Plants native to your area will be best for wildlife. These plants are the food sources and shelter that local wildlife can use best. As well as the pretties and those obviously good for wildlife, don't forget to add oxygenators to help keep the water clear – you buy these by the bundle and need to put about 15 stems in for every square metre of pond surface area you have.

6 **Keeping it clear** Murky, smelly ponds are the second biggest reason that people have for not wanting a pond in the garden (the main reason is concern about safety). Algae feed on nutrients in the water and need sunlight to flourish. So clearing out weeds, leaves and excess fish food will help keep the water free of nutrients. To help keep out sunlight make sure a large proportion of the top surface is covered by planting.

▲ Rice paper plant　　　▲ Tree fern　　　▲ Aeonium　　　▲ Honey bush　　　▲ Canna lilies

Exotic heat islands

This is the name Angus White from Architectural Plants gives to the potential of gardens in large cities. He comes up with some startling statistics: for example, the minimum temperature in London in winter is comparable to the south coast of France. OK, it's hotter in the summer in France, but it's the minimum temperature that is important for plants' survival and happiness. On one of the coldest nights in recent history in 1991, Angus recorded a temperature of minus 17°C in West Sussex. In London on the same night the minimum was minus 4°C, an enormous 13° difference. This 'heat island' effect is huge and its benefits are little exploited.

It's not just London; in any city area the buildings and roads absorb heat during the day and release it at night. Add to this central heating, cars and people, and you have an enormous amount of heat being generated – the larger the city the more extreme this will be.

Angus has understandable caveats about suggesting going for very tender plants. If there's one thing we can predict about the British weather, it's that it's unpredictable. But do try a few less hardy plants and see how you get on.

▲ Ginger lilies   ▲ Black banana   ▲ Red Cestrum   ▲ Variegated soapwort   ▲ Mexican blue palm

10

top tropicals

1 **Rice paper plant.** A wonderful, tall plant with huge palm-shaped leaves. It can sucker, so you need to put in an underground barrier sheet to stop it spreading.

2 **Tree fern.** Probably the most common of the jungle-like tender plants, this is everywhere, but it's everywhere because it's such a nice plant.

3 **Aeonium.** Happy in a pot, the black version slowly, slowly grows into interesting shapes.

4 **Honey bush.** This is pretty hardy and has blue-green cut leaves. It will probably die back in winter but come up again next year.

5 **Canna lilies.** With purple leaves and orange flowers, these tall plants are wonderful for late summer colour.

6 **Ginger lily.** Spectacular orange flowers and beautiful foliage.

7 **Black banana.** These provide some of the most tropical-looking foliage, don't expect any fruit though!

8 **Red Cestrum.** Evergreen with red flowers in summer.

9 **Variegated soapwort.** This variegated soapwort isn't as hardy as the all green one, but is more interesting.

10 **Mexican blue palm.** With silvery blue fan-shaped leaves, this can go wonderfully well with canna lilies. It likes full sun.

▲ A hidden room at the bottom of the garden by English Garden Carpentry Company is just the right place to escape to – this is the 21st-century take on the garden shed!

▲ Fletcher and Myburgh do the most wonderful creations – to call them 'seats' doesn't do them justice. This one is a perfect place to hideaway in a smaller garden.

Hideaways

Hideaways in the garden are the essence of what a family garden is about – they're fun and they provide an escape, a place to think. And that goes as much for adults as for children. The den in this garden is just that. For the children it becomes a pirate ship or a castle, and the adults can find some peace to sit and read or just sit.

▲ The child-sized tepees from Urchin make wonderful dens and look good in the garden as well.

▲ This is a tipi that's big enough for adults as well as children - it's by Wigwam Sam who makes and hires out all sizes and types of tipis.

▲ Lying in a tepee looking up at the shadows of trees. Feeling the warmth of the sun, diluted through the sides, but still gently bringing out the scent of the grass. A great experience for children (and adults). This is one of Wigwam Sam's.

▲ Treehouses have real family appeal – they act as dens, climbing frames and springboards for children's imagination. But they are also great places for adults to relax and hide. These are both by treehouselife.

10

Rendered Walls

DESIGN BRIEF
- **Link with the new extension**
- **Include a lawn**
- **Be practical**

FEATURES
- **Rendered and painted walls**
- **Water feature**
- **Seating area at rear**

'If you have walls just for the sake of it, it looks dumb, there has to be a reason to have them there.' Paula Ryan, the designer here, has made low, free-standing walls something of a trademark and she uses them with skill. These walls define, divide, hide and more.

This is quite a long garden and one of the walls' primary purposes here is to widen the garden out and form punctuation marks as the eye journeys down it. 'The client was very keen to have a lawn and the path to the left of it was making something of a runway. Your eye went straight to the back without stopping, but the walls give horizontal lines to the garden and stop your eye from travelling straight down.'

Water feature At the rear a water feature provides the main focal point of the garden.

Walls The walls provide strong horizontal lines to mitigate the visual effects of the long path to the side. They provide sharp, clean lines in contrast to the diaphanous planting and they define different areas of the garden.

Lights Uplighters are used to make shadows on the walls.

Flooring On the floor are granite and concrete. This gives a light, almost Mediterranean feel to the terrace.

Trees Existing trees give wonderful shade and maturity to the garden and provide an ideal spot for a hanging chair.

Holes Most cleverly the holes in the walls lighten their dominance and allows glimpses through to the planting behind. Imagine this scene where the walls were solid: they would overpower the whole look of the garden.

▲ **Lines of containers** with box in them finish off the look of the terrace.

▲ **The strong** framework of the walls means that this loose planting can work.

▲ **Granite blocks** surrounded with bark chips mark a change to a less formal part of the garden.

▲ **One of my** favourite elements of the garden is the trellis work next to the terrace. Simple but beautiful, three screens of horizontal slats of pine are held between bold, white uprights.

▲ **A gap** in the wall takes the weight out of the wall and is used as a shelf for candles. If this wall had been solid it would have made the terrace feel very enclosed.

'The overall design for this garden had to reflect a very modern new interior that was, as Paula says, "so crisp and white, we had to link this in with the garden". By using the white walls the design has taken that crispness into the garden and made a useable and useful space. And because the walls have achieved that, there was no need to be minimalist in the planting. This contrast of airy planting with the stark white structure of the walls brings this garden to life.'

Design

The design here looks quite complex with lots of different areas and bits jutting out. But a repetition of forms and of materials holds it all together, so that on the ground it appears unified and simple.

Large shed for storage, hidden behind high wall

Water feature held by wall

Seating area to catch evening sun

Path down garden

Lawn to the side of the garden

Existing tree to remain

Existing tree to remain

Large terrace with beige granite and poured concrete on the floor

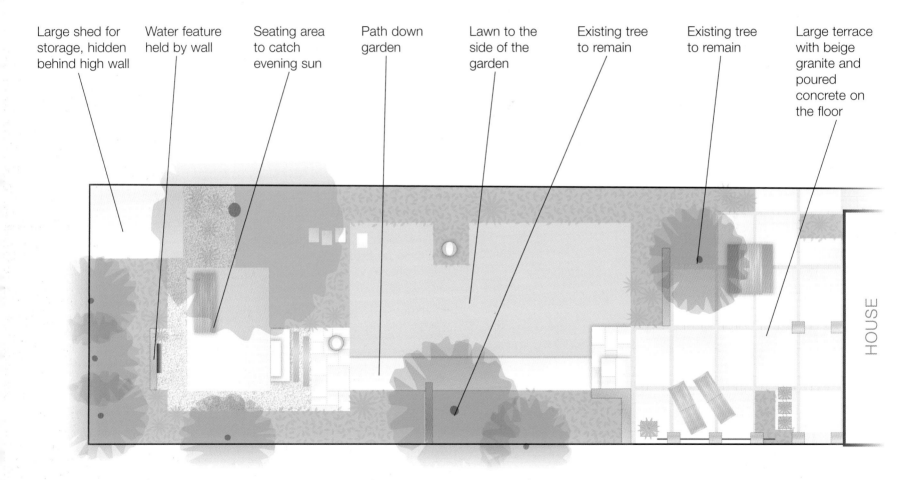

HOUSE

0　1　2　3 metres

10
uses of free-standing walls

1 Divide
Like any screen, walls can be used to form actual or implied boundaries to divide up areas.

2 Interest
Often walls are used like flats on a stage to punctuate the scene as it moves away from the eye.

3 Structure
Walls can provide very strong horizontal and vertical lines to the garden.

4 Hide
Solid and potentially tall, walls are great for completely masking any unsightly and unwanted features.

5 Built-in seating
Walls can hold seats. The horizontal line of modern inbuilt-in seating looks beautifully sculptural against a flat plane.

6 Planting backdrop
The colour of the wall is important for this. There are no rules and part of the fun is experimenting with colour, but contrasts are always a good place to start. If the wall is light coloured try brightly coloured plants and vice-versa.

7 Shadows
Whether you use sunlight or uplighters, bold planting or unstructured, the effects of shadow play on the flat surface of a wall are magical.

8 Display
In this garden the wall provides the perfect surround to a modern water feature, but walls can also be used to define and 'hold' sculpture in the garden.

9 Seats
Placed at the right height walls can make extra, uncluttered seating or, if higher, a bar to lean against, look over and contemplate the world.

10 Contrasts
This is where walls come into their own. The starkness and purity of their lines plays so well in a garden setting where they can be placed against exuberant or architectural planting.

Shadows and shapes

Shadows aren't the first thing you think about when you're designing a garden or choosing plants. But if you do consider this aspect, and if you get it right, the effects can be magical. Modern gardens with plain, sleek surfaces are ideal for casting shadows onto or for really showing up the shapes of plants, but even a well-cut lawn will give a wonderful display of dancing lights from the sunlight coming through a tree.

You need to know a garden quite well to know how the light works at various times of the year and at different times of the day, but it's worth taking the time to watch and capture the light.

Watching the light is a useful thing to do, not just for creating pretty shadows – you might want to make sure that play frames are in the shade in summer, or that there's somewhere to sit at the end of the evening to catch the last rays of sunshine.

5

ideas for wall design

Cut-outs
In this garden the holes are rectangles. But you can also have circular, oval or freeform holes and gaps. These will lighten the wall and can be viewing holes or places to shine lights through or just to look good.

Niches
The holes don't have to go all the way through the wall. Niches can be created in the wall for sitting or for placing sculpture, or they can be just painted a different colour.

Curves
Walls can curve, snake about or form almost complete circles to enclose an area.

Columns
Walls don't have to be long. Tall columns can be used to define an area and provide a strong, repeated pattern.

Surface
Most of the walls in this book are rendered and painted. This gives a clean, modern canvas. Where it can be less than successful is with the capping along the top: put the wrong capping on and it won't look modern. To avoid the 'hacienda' look and get a really clean line, avoid using anything even remotely rustic – and that includes bricks. Only use the sleekest stone or avoid the issue altogether and use beading at the edges of the wa instead.

Rendering a wall Tim Fitch, a builder with nearly 20 years' experience, talks us through the jargon and explains how to render a wall.

1 These special bits of metal mesh are called 'profiles' and they help to get a really good sharp edge and corner to the render. You fix them to the wall with galvanised wire nails.

2 This is render going on. it's a paste made up of sand, cement and a little mortar plasticiser. You put a small amount onto the hand-held table called a 'hawk' and use a trowel to spread it. Work from the base up.

3 As you're working in the render in an arc, the trailing edge of the trowel should be the only surface in contact with the wall. Too flat and the trowel will stick and pull off a large section of the newly applied render.

4 The plasterer's darby. A straight edge that is drawn up the wall to collect and scrape off the high points of the trowel-applied render. There's going to be a second coat of render so make sure you're not going right out to the edge of the plastering profiles.

Practical matters

- You may need planning permission to build a wall so it's best to ask first.
- Rendered and painted walls will need regular maintenance.

- Walls are a major construction in the garden and one which can cause huge damage if they are built incorrectly; if in doubt, get specialist advice.

5 The plasterer's scratching tool. This just makes lines in the first coat of render to provide a physical adhesive key for the second coat, when it is applied. The first coat needs to set but not dry out.

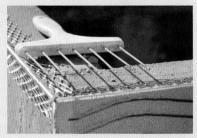

6 The second and final coat of render has the same pocess as the first but instead of scratching the surface at the end you use a plasterer's float just as the render is starting to set to get a really flat surface.

7 Use a moist sponge to get the final texture.

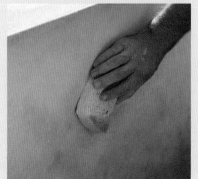

8 Job done.

Roof Garden

DESIGN BRIEF
- **A garden in the sky**
- **Two seating areas**
- **Shelter from the wind**

FEATURES
- **Raised beds**
- **Water feature**
- **Metal floor grille**

This roof garden had to be a garden – not a terrace, not a balcony. The designer Philip Nash's aim was to 'create a garden that could have been on the ground, and lift it on to the roof'.

Having said that, it's not just a back garden on high, there is plenty in the garden that cleverly takes into account the problems of roof gardens and at the same time makes the most of the views.

Screening from wind and bad views There's a tension in the design of roof gardens: on the one hand you need protection from the wind, but on the other you want to make the most of the best views. Here tall planting has been used on the side that receives the prevailing winds; fortunately it is also the side with the least good views. So, as if by magic, the seats are nestled into a cosy corner, protected by the wind but with the best views out.

Water feature At the centre of the garden is a water feature designed and built by Philip. Within the garden the eye is led to the water feature by metal grating that runs from the entrance straight there.

Raised beds Around the built-in seating area and the pond are raised beds with lush, architectural planting. Yuccas and bamboos give height and a feeling of enclosure, which is so important to creating the atmosphere of this garden.

Built-in seats Hidden under the seats are lighting and speakers for a sound system, controlled from inside the house. The speakers are waterproof and intended for outdoor use, but putting them under the seats prevents the sound being lost to the air.

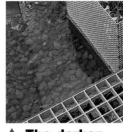

▲ **Water flows** up through the triangular column and over the top. A light inside shows through the cut-out design.

▲ **The darker the pond,** the better the reflections will be. The dark pebbles here help to reflect the sky.

▲ **The planting** is used for form and texture rather than for flowers.

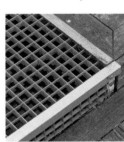

▲ **To keep the weight down,** the raised beds are made of outdoor marine ply with a support frame. The pebbles also have another use: they cover the lining at the bottom

▲ **Low steps** have been incorporated into the design to help define different areas and raise up the floor level, so the pond can sit flush with 'ground' level.

▲ **Designs at 45 degrees** immediately give a dynamic to what might be a fairly straightforward division of the space.

'There's nothing delicate or unsure about this garden. The planting is architectural and robust enough to withstand the elements. The lines of the garden also are clear and strong. And the technical design is accomplished. Making a garden and making it work are very difficult in circumstances such as this, but there's a real synergy here between the practical, technical demands of the site and the need for an aesthetically pleasing garden. On top of those technical demands, Philip has created an atmosphere rather than just decorated a space; it is, most definitely, a garden.'

Design

Putting the design at 45° gives a dynamic feel to this design and allows for built-in seats to look out to the sides, not back to the entrance. Also placing the water feature off centre takes the eye right across the garden as you enter and makes it seem larger.

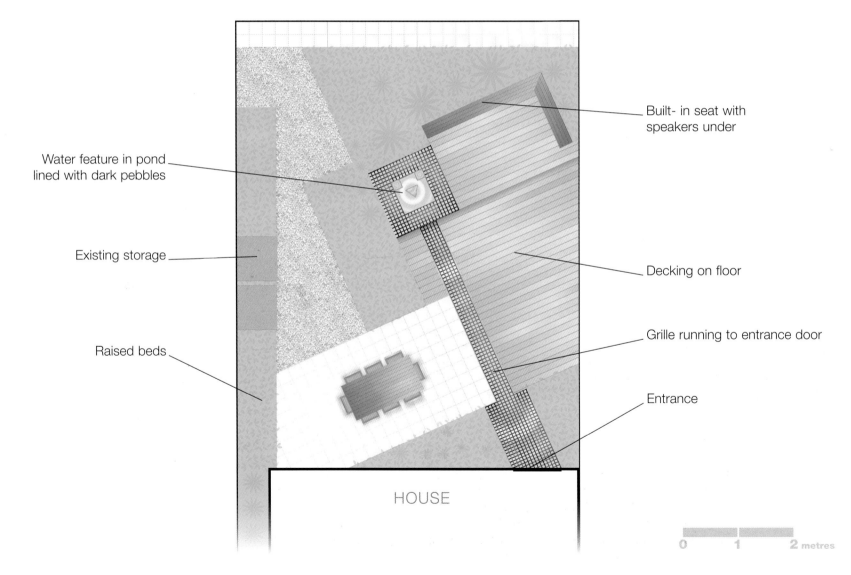

Built- in seat with speakers under

Water feature in pond lined with dark pebbles

Existing storage

Raised beds

Decking on floor

Grille running to entrance door

Entrance

HOUSE

0   1   2 metres

8

tips for roof gardens

I'm sure there are worse places to create a garden, but a roof has to be up there on the list. Drying winds, lack of shade, weight restrictions and no soil – it's a wonder anyone tries at all. But since the hanging gardens of Babylon, roof gardens have proved that they can be magical spaces. Although the design possibilities are limitless, there are some basic aspects to consider:

1 Regulations may have an impact on what you want to do. Building regulations stipulate the type of barrier around the garden and also what you can have on the floor. It's worth checking to see if you need planning permission as well.

2 If you have a roof that might be turned into a garden, the first thing to do is get in an architect or structural engineer to talk about weight and whether your roof can stand having plants, soil, floor material and people on it.

3 Apart from weight restrictions, another problem is the potential for strong winds. Any trellis will have to be attached well and plants anchored in. And to make the area more useable, it's worth finding out where the prevailing wind comes from and forming a suitable screen.

4 Whether you want a lush or minimalist garden, if you have plants you will have to use containers of some sort. To create atmosphere with dense planting raised beds will probably work best, but they are heavier and more expensive. Smaller containers and pots are easier to put in, but dry out more quickly and can get blown over.

5 Whatever type of container you have the plants will need a lot of water. Containers, because of their limited soil, will hold less water than the ground. Add to this the drying effects of the wind and an irrigation system begins to look like a worthwhile labour saver. Whether you water by hand or automatically, make sure excess water can drain away and safely off the roof.

6 As in this garden, it's a good idea to save on weight by using polystyrene or perlite instead of soil at the bottom of the containers. A peat substitute is lighter than ordinary loam-based compost.

7 If you're using raised beds, make sure the roots of the plants are contained well within the beds. If you have smaller containers, check occasionally to make sure the roots haven't worked their way out and into the roof.

8 Both the user and the environment can gain enormous benefits from roof gardens. They create green spaces in urban environments, help to remove carbon dioxide, insulate the building below, and can be enormous fun.

DESIGNER'S TIP

Strangely, solid screens are not ideal. In any situation where you're trying to cut down wind a semi-permeable screen will work best. You want to slow the wind, not stop it and force it up and over the top and, inevitably, down again.

Screening

Plants are great at providing a barrier between you and the world. A single plant will do – plant a few in a row and you have a hedge.

What hedge?

One of the first things to decide when planting a hedge is whether you want an evergreen hedge or a deciduous one, and do you want a screen all year round or something that changes with the seasons and may not be much of a screen at all in the winter?

Then you might want to decide whether you want something formal, with sleek straight lines that you can cut to precise shapes; or something informal, a little fuzzy but interesting. The main deciding factor for this is the way the plant grows. Plants with very tight growth and small leaves are the best for creating those razor-sharp lines. Plants that flop and have quite lax growth are never going to be cajoled into geometry.

Hedges

DECIDUOUS

Deciduous informal

Hawthorn
- Great for wildlife
- Blossom and berries to give a change through the year
- Has thorns so good for deterring burglars
- Quite slow growing
- Plant at 30 centimetres apart
- Also try roses: the sweet briar rose makes a lovely hedge with pink flowers in summer and lovely red hips in autumn

Deciduous formal

Beech or copper beech
- Lovely autumn colour
- Dead leaves are held over winter so there is some protection
- Need to cut off a third of the plant when it first goes in the ground to get the best growth
- Plant 45 centimetres apart
- Also try purple hazel

How to plant a hedge

Usually with hedges you buy them 'bare root' – quite literally they are dug out of the ground in the nursery, the soil is shaken off and they are sold to you. Bare root plants are only available in winter when the leaves are off deciduous plants (like beech and hornbeam). The deciduous plants are fine with the disruption at that time of year, and even evergreens can tolerate being handled this way in the winter, but treat them gently, and keep the roots covered and moist even if they're not in the ground.

You can buy your plants in containers, but they will be more expensive, and when you're doing a hedge and might need 50 or so plants the extra cost of each individual plant can mount up. However, in a container the plants are available and can be planted all year round (as long as the ground's not frozen or the weather's so hot they will be too stressed and thirsty).

EVERGREEN

Evergreen informal

Holly
- Comes in many different types with different-coloured leaves and berries
- Prickly so good for deterring burglars
- Berries are good for wildlife
- Quite slow growing
- Plant at 45 centimetres apart
- Also try cherry laurel, with its large, glossy green leaves

Evergreen formal

There are lots of plants to make a formal evergreen hedge. This is the main type of hedging that people want, basically a green wall.

Yew

The queen of hedges, this can be cut to within an inch of its life. It can be shaped into lines so sharp you can cut yourself and once it starts growing nothing is going to get through its dense growth. It's also a good low- maintenance plant: if you cut it after the middle of August it only needs one cut a year. Compare this to privet, which can need trimming two or three times.

Box

Another great evergreen with tight growth and small leaves. The only trouble with box is that, if you want a decent - sized hedge, you need to plant it when you're about 15 to enjoy in your old age. (I'm exaggerating, but it will be about 10 years before it gets to 6 feet!). You can buy big plants but, because it's box is so slow growing, thesre are really expensive,: you're paying for a nursery to have looked after and housed the plants for a decade. Nevertheless, box is great for low hedges.

Privet

Privet is a good evergreen plant, but it's kind of boring. And why, if you could plant dramatic, dark green yew, would you want to put in so-so green privet? It also takes more looking after and needs to be cut at least twice a year.

1. Dig a trench large enough to take the roots with ease. Use string and a tape measure to get a straight line.

2. Work up the soil in the bottom to help the roots get a foothold.

3. Put the plants in and cover round the roots with soil. Make sure the plant is planted at the same depth as it has been in the field

– you will see the colour change on the stem. Really firm the plants in so there aren't any big air pockets. Use a measure to make sure the plants are an equal distance apart.

4. With deciduous plants (such as beech) cut off a third of the top growth just after you've

planted them. This will encourage them to bush out.

▲ Sedums are the natural choice for extensive systems - they are there all year round and don't mind if there is a dry spell in the summer. These where photographed on a green roof by Blackdown Horticultural Consultants Limited.

▲ In a smart move towards complete outdoor living – put the kitchen outside along with the dining area! This roof garden complete with outside sink is by Urban Roof Gardens.

▲ Even small roof gardens can make a great outside room – just enough space to lie back and relax. This one is by Urban Roof Gardens.

▲ Green roofs work wonderfully well on slightly sloping roofs. This one, by Blackdown Horticultural Consultants Limited, helps to blend the building into the surroundings.

▼ Covering the barriers with stylish planters and strong foliage is a good place to start with a roof garden. This one uses copper planters and is by Urban Roof Gardens.

What is a green roof?

If there are plants on the roof, it's a green roof. The plants could be sedums or even moss, and they can be planted in a way that couldn't by any means count as a garden, with no real access for people. At the other end of the scale there are full-blown gardens on high with trees, shrubs, seats, the works.

There's a little bit of jargon that the people who do green roofs use:

Intensive systems are gardens on roofs. They might have trees and seating areas, anything you would find in a garden at ground level. With all these plants and access they need a depth of soil or some growing medium and enough strength to be safe for people to use.

Extensive systems are low maintenance, with a 'self-sustaining plant community'. You have these for the way the roof looks, for the sake of the building and for the environment, rather than for use as a garden.

What's so good about a green roof?
- Insulation – it helps with the heat insulation of the building.
- Sound reduction – it protects the building from noise.
- Protection – it shields the roof surface from ultraviolet rays.
- Decreases flood risk by soaking up rainwater.
- The water instead travels through the plants and is released back into the air and acts as a natural coolant.
- Improves the air quality by soaking up carbon dioxide, releasing oxygen and water vapour, and absorbing organic volatiles.
- Provides a habitat for birds and insects.

6

questions about green roofs

Karen Tarr from Blackdown Horticultural Consultants Limited, specialists in green roofs, answers some questions about green roofs.

Q **Don't they let water into the building?**

A. No, quite the opposite in fact. A correctly installed green roof system will prolong the life of the waterproofing by protecting it from ultraviolet rays and the elements. It is important that the waterproofing is thoroughly checked and renewed if necessary prior to installing the green roof.

Q **Isn't the whole thing really heavy with soil and water?**

A. We don't use soil; we use special lightweight growing mediums that retain just enough water for the plants. Plants like sedums require only shallow growing medium for their roots, which helps to keep the weight down too. The deeper the growing medium needed (for shrubs and even trees), the more the whole planting will weigh.

Q **Isn't it difficult to install and look after?**

A. Provided it's the green roof has been well planned it should be quite straightforward to put in and the extensive systems are specially designed to be low maintenance. Like any new planting it needs watching for weeds in its first year, but after that it's generally a once-a-year job.

Q **What happens after five or ten years?**

A. If correctly designed and with minimal maintenance, the green roof should last for many years and prolong the life of the roof's waterproofing considerably.

Q **Why do you use sedums?**

A. They are particularly suited to the tough conditions on the roof: they are evergreen, self-generating and drought resistant. A slight increase in the depth of the substrate will support other plants like certain types of primulas, iris, *Dianthus* and *Potentillas*. With a further increase in the depth of the substrate, more upright species such as grasses and wildflowers can be used.

Q **If you've got a sloping roof, can you still have a green roof?**

A. You actually need a bit of a slope to allow water to run off (between two and eight degrees is ideal) and we have developed successful methods of preventing slippage in steeper roofs, although these can be more expensive to install.

With a slightly deeper growing medium it's possible to create a colourful meadow effect, this one is by Blackdown Horticultural Consultants Limited.

12

Oriental

DESIGN BRIEF
- **Create a good view, day and night**
- **Somewhere to sit**
- **Act as an extension of house**

FEATURES
- **Raised bed for shrubs**
- **Architectural sculpture**
- **Coloured glass light fittings**

This garden was created when the owners of the town house converted the building at the back of their land into a sitting room with bedroom above. The garden, which was already small, suddenly shrank.

The new sitting room extended out and ate away at the back of the space. A covered walkway was built to link the house to the new rooms and the space was cut back even further. What was left was a tiny, sunken area surrounded on all sides by walls. The owner, who designed the garden, was happy to compromise on the size of the garden: 'The garden had to be big enough to enjoy but given our weather we opted for increased indoor space.'

The tiny space left could have been a cause for despair. But what's been created is a lovely, leafy hideaway courtyard, which at night comes alive with lighting. The key here is having a theme.

Walkway A glass-covered walkway links the new rooms to the back with the main house.

Lighting Lighting is key to this garden: hanging lights and spotlights give an exciting oriental feeling.

Sculpture Hidden in the greenery are pieces of sculpture, so even in a tiny space like this there is a surprise.

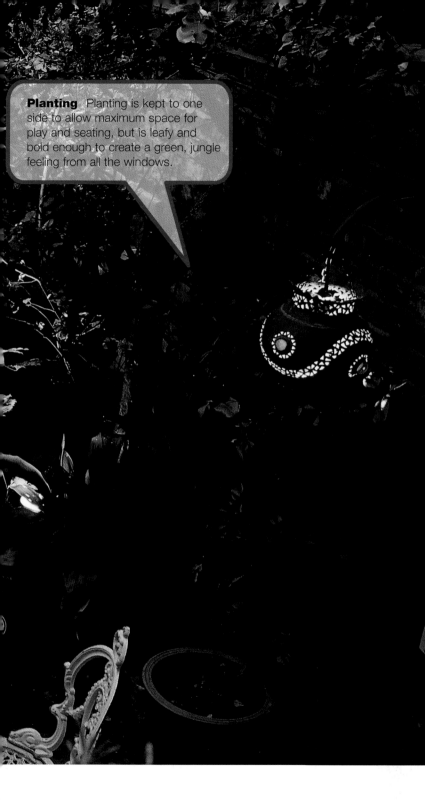

> **Planting** Planting is kept to one side to allow maximum space for play and seating, but is leafy and bold enough to create a green, jungle feeling from all the windows.

▲ **The doors** to the new sitting room open right back so the distinction between inside and out is blurred.

▲ **Tiny details** such as these inlaid stones add to the quirky feel of the garden.

◀ ▲ **The sculptures** are huge in this small space, but they fit with the large leaves of the jungle planting like remnants of a lost world of giants.

> *'I didn't want anything fake, it's a matter of applying touches to add flavour, to create a look.'*

Design

Before the corridor and extension at the rear were built this was a tiny garden. With both of these now in place, what's left is miniscule. The key here is to keep all the planting along one wall. It is lush and quite a dominant part of the views out to the garden, but it's contained and so the garden is usable.

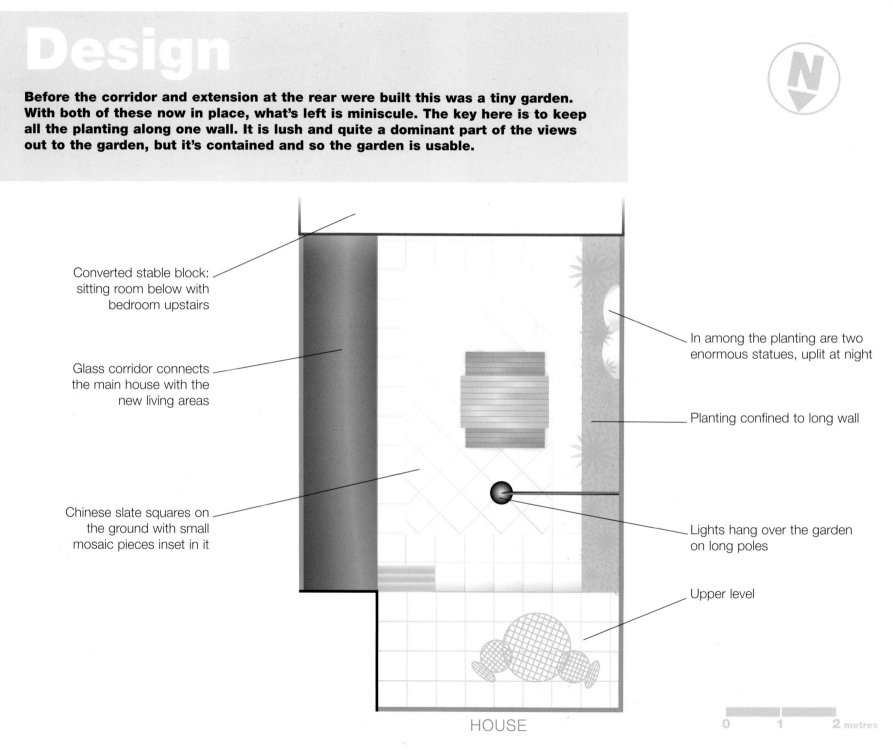

Converted stable block: sitting room below with bedroom upstairs

Glass corridor connects the main house with the new living areas

Chinese slate squares on the ground with small mosaic pieces inset in it

In among the planting are two enormous statues, uplit at night

Planting confined to long wall

Lights hang over the garden on long poles

Upper level

HOUSE

0   1   2 metres

Extensions

Writing this book and also doing garden designs for people, it has struck me that one of the main reasons for needing to rethink a garden is having an extension built onto the back of the house. It's a wonderful opportunity to look at the way both the inside and the outside spaces are used and to make them work together.

5 tips to make garden and extension work together

1 Movement between inside and out One of the main benefits of creating a new area at the rear is having easy access in and out of the garden. In traditional houses access to the rear garden wasn't a priority and was often a side door or a small door up steps. Now we want an easy transition between house and garden to encourage movement between the two.

2 Proportions Extending the house out can dramatically alter the proportions of the garden – sometimes for the better. A long, thin space suddenly becomes a shorter, more pleasant area to be in. But at other times, the extension can create problems, especially on a sloping site.

3 Balance Rather than matching inside and out, you can go for balance and reflect the new extension in the garden without following the style – so the two link and form part of the same set-up, but aren't one big room.

4 Views New extensions tend to have lots of windows, often floor to ceiling, so the views out become very important. What's more, you'll be seeing the garden all through the year, so the picture in winter is as important as the picture in summer.

5 Matching out and in When glass walls can be flung back to blur the line between inside and out, it's great if the two spaces can feel as one. So clean white walls can be mirrored outside, and similar furniture and decoration can be used. One of the most important ways to get the two to blend is to use the same materials on the floor inside and out. One thing about all of this: the extension will really dictate how the garden looks if you go down this route. This might be just what you want – on the other hand, you may want to have something radically different outside.

One further note: if you don't want to change your garden to fit your new extension, you can build the extension around your garden … you can bring the outside in. The existing tree has dictated the shape and form of this extension.

▲ Lace-cap hydrangea

▲ Bush ivy

▲ Launistinus

Plants for shade

In this garden the plants need to work very hard: it's a small, shady place and the garden needs to look good all year round.

The camellia and Japanese aralia have beautiful glossy green leaves and will survive in the darkest corner, while above them, reaching for the light, is flannel bush 'California Glory', a semi-hardy wall shrub that produces yellow flowers in spring and autumn. The Chusan palm gives a spiky feel to the lower planting.

7

shade lovers

Opposite is a list of seven plants for a shady courtyard that will give year-round interest. The planting list starts with the tall, structural plans and also includes suggestions for middle and lower layer plants for seasonal interest.

▲ White bluebells

▲ Japanese painted fern

▲ Masterwort

1 Launistinus Quite a large evergreen shrub with late winter white flowers.

2 Bush ivy It looks like an ivy with enormous evergreen leaves and it is related to ivy, but it will need help to climb. You need to tie bush ivy in to wires to encourage it to go up.

3 Hydrangeas Their light-coloured flowers, which come out towards the end of the summer, work incredibly well in shady courtyards. Lace-cap ones have more delicate flowers.

4 Geraniums Wonderfully forgiving plants that can tolerate all sorts of conditions and give a great display of both leaf and flower through the summer and into autumn.

5 Masterwort These are lovely intricate little flowers early in the summer. And if you cut them back when they start to die off they may flower again.

6 Bulbs Many bulbs will be happy in a shady spot. Look for the spring-flowering bulbs like snowdrops, winter aconites or hyacinths.

7 Ferns Most ferns will be happy in low light and even low rainfall. A particularly good one for shade is a Japanese painted fern (*Athyrium niponicum*), which is quite big and showy and, because it has silver highlights, really lights up a dark area.

▲ Geranium

Sculpture

Sculpture is one of those areas where children's and adults' needs can merge together beautifully. Adults can bring art, fun and a sense of the unexpected into their gardens, and children can have the most thrilling, stimulating environment.

Making stuff yourself

It's possible to be very creative in the garden and allow your artistic side out, much more so than inside. Why not try to make a concrete sculpture by digging a hole and making a formwork (a wooden 'mould') and pouring the concrete in? Why not use painted marine ply to make a shelter or a sculpture?

In this garden the sculptures were designed by the owner and his friend. They're created from polystyrene, made into a mould, and the final sculpture is coated in a mix of limestone powder so it has the appearance of real stone.

The owner has also been creative with the lights: the main light was adapted from a candle holder. He used opaque Perspex to line the inside of the holder to hide his newly fitted light bulb and fixed the whole thing to a pole hanging over the garden.

DESIGNER'S TIP

Objects that challenge the scale of a space, especially if stumbled on in the garden, are great fun. Fallen columns, industrial salvage or items from agricultural auctions can all be used to make sculpture. Lit at night, their forms can take on a completely different air.least suggest an alternative.

In this garden by George Carter, he has adapted a ballcock from a toilet, spray-painted it gold and put it on top of a water feature.

George has also made simple garden shelters and ornaments from trelliswork.

An incredibly easy piece of sculpture: just three stones, perfectly balanced, lie hidden among the greenery.

▲ Even a humble birdbath can be a thing of real beauty. This one, designed to sink into the ground, is from Metallic Garden.

◀ A large stainless steel sculpture from Steinworks cuts through the feathery foliage around it.

These are ▶ 'metots' designed by a company called Garden Totems to catch the wind and move and sway like tall grasses in the garden.

◀ Putting this small modern sculpture into the flower bed makes the most of the contrast between its modern lines and the foliage around it. This smaller piece is by Steinworks sculpture.

It doesn't have to be 'art' to be fun: here sheets of Perspex have been covered with coloured film and placed in wooden frames to provide an exciting, multicoloured maze.

DESIGNER'S TIP

Shows by students are great places to buy sculpture. The pieces are inexpensive and you help to encourage someone who is starting out.

This little ▶ sculpture (just 40cm tall) from Ambient Home and Garden is hand carved from limestone and looks lovely nestled in tall grass or amongst flowers.

13

Wildlife Garden

DESIGN BRIEF
- **Encourage bees, hoverflies and butterflies**
- **Work with the environment and the soil**

FEATURES
- **Borders arranged like hedgerows**
- **Small wildlife pond**
- **Wild bee houses**

A wildlife garden in South London? It's not the most obvious place to devote a garden to the natural world but, as we stand underneath a hawthorn and our voices are drowned out not by wailing sirens but by birdsong and our discussion is interrupted by a nosy fox, I begin to see the point.

'Hedgerow' design The design of this area replicates the natural form of hedgerows, with long lines of planted areas to give maximum cover to small creatures.

Plants The borders are filled with plants that have nectar and will encourage bees. Plants are grouped into drifts that carry on across the central path.

Grass path The grass path needs to be kept well mown to set off the naturalistic planting and give the area structure. If the grass were left long the garden would look too much like a wilderness.

Hawthorn Above is a hawthorn, which has berries for the birds to eat and will provide cover for their nests. Its thorns will help to keep out cats as well. This idea of a tree layer, a hedgerow layer and, at the bottom, an understorey imitates the way plants would be found in the countryside.

Ground cover There's no bare soil in the garden – so there's no place for unwelcome weeds to find a foothold. Again, this is exactly how plants would grow in the wild.

▲ **Although not all natives,** the plants have been chosen to fit with the environment and with the different conditions found within the garden.

▲ **Late summer plants** are great for wild bees: they extend the season when the bees can be active and collect nectar.

▲ **The pond** has a beach of pebbles for frogs to come in and out of the pond.

▲ **The dead hedge** is a great 'labour saver'. Marc Carlton, the garden's owner, lays any long twigs and prunings across the top. As he says, 'It means you don't have to have bonfires or take them to the tip. They rot down so it never fills up.'

◄ **The bee houses** in the garden are perfect for wild solitary bees, with lots of different-sized holes for various types of bees to lay their eggs in. These bees are stingless, completely harmless and important pollinators of fruit trees and bushes.

'This garden is a complete labour of love, but based on a deep understanding of the natural world Marc is able to offer up some simple and foolproof ideas to encourage wildlife into any garden.'

Design

The garden used to be split into two and that history is apparent in the design. In each area a different type of planting is used to work with the specific conditions.

Wildlife pond

Copse area of native shrubs

Vegetable area

Pollinator border

Wild bee house

Wildflower lawn

Grass path through deep borders of plants

Raised decking

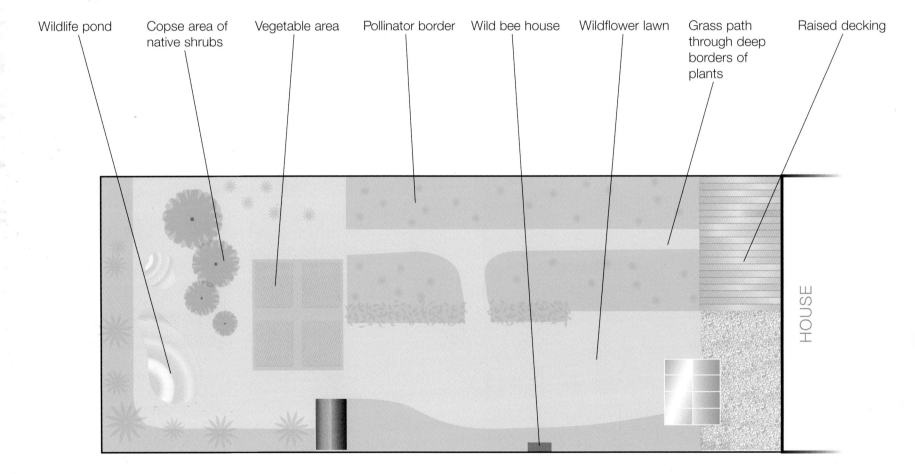

HOUSE

0 1 2 3 4 5 metres

Encouraging wildlife

Mark Carlton, the owner of this garden, is passionate about encouraging wildlife. He has a wonderful website where you can find out more about the garden and about encouraging wildlife into your garden – visit www.foxleas.com. Here he answers some questions about wildlife in the garden.

Q What sort of things should you plant in the garden if you want to attract bees and butterflies?

A. It's difficult to use just wildflowers in the garden, but plant varieties that are close to their wild ancestors, like old-fashioned cottage garden plants, are good.

Q Do you have to plant natives?

A. What's a native? Not long ago we were attached to mainland Europe and our wildlife can make use of many plant species from the rest of Europe. Plant species from further afield, North America and the southern hemisphere, tend to be less useful.

Q Why is that?

A. One major reason: a lot of flowers from those places are bird pollinated and so are red. Birds see the colour red very well, but bees (our pollinators) don't so the red flowers are effectively invisible to them. An exception is flowers like poppies and red roses that reflect ultraviolet light, which bees can see.

Q What else should you avoid planting if you want to attract bees and butterflies?

A. Double flowers aren't good at all, in most cases the stamens (which would carry the pollen) have been developed into petals.

Q How should the plants be arranged?

A. The idea we've got here is that the plants should recreate the roles they would have in nature: the tree layer, the hedgerow layer and the understorey. Much of our wildlife in the country depends on the hedgerow layer, both for food and shelter but also for a safe way to move around the area. So I've recreated in the long borders a hedgerow type of environment. Also everything is really densely planted, just as it would be in the wild, so the plants provide a continuous shelter for animals and we don't get many weeds, as there's no room for them.

Q If you had to chose one plant?

A. Wild marjoram. It is wonderful for attracting bees and butterflies and has a long flowering period.

Q Why should gardeners care about bees?

A. Because gardeners can really help their conservation. For example, there are 25 species of bumblebee in the UK, 18 of which are threatened and two have become extinct already. About six species are still doing well and that's as a direct result of gardens and gardeners' activities.

Q Why do we need wild bees?

A. For vegetables and fruit trees and even farm crops, bees of all kinds are needed as pollinators.

Creating a wildflower meadow

It is possible to create a wildflower meadow in a small garden. The lawn here is being developed as one and it is a wonderful thing to do for wildlife.

REASONS TO CREATE A WILDFLOWER MEADOW

YES

- It's great for wildlife, providing both food and cover.
- There's an ever-changing gallery of different plants.
- It means you don't have to mow the lawn for a good part of the year.
- Children can lie in the long grass, hidden from view.
- Your lawn will come alive with the humming of all sorts of insects: bumblebees, hoverflies and butterflies.
- It's unpredictable.

NO

- It's a long, slow process to create a real wildflower meadow and it relies on the soil being starved of nutrients so the thuggish weeds – docks and nettles – don't take over.
- It also requires a bit of space: grass you don't need to use for sitting or games for a fair bit of the year.
- It's unpredictable.

If you still want to go ahead

- You need to get rid of as many nutrients as possible. Either quickly by taking off the topsoil or slowly, by every time you cut the grass taking away the cuttings and with them the nutrients. Over the years the soil will become more and more depleted.
- You can sow seed or use plugs (very small plants supplied in containers a bit like egg boxes) or just let nature take its course. Marc recommends plugs.
- If you need to find out what sort of plants would be native to you, you can either ask a supplier of plugs or you can go to www.nhm.ac.uk/science/projects/fff, the postcode plants database. Put in your postcode and the site will tell you what plants are local to your area.

Maintenance of a wildflower area

1. Keep cutting the grass from July through to March. Marc is adamant that you should cut it and keep cutting it from July onwards, even if it means cutting down flowers. 'If you let the grass bulk up through the summer it will take over from the delicate wildflowers.'
2. Make sure you always take off the cuttings.

There is another way

If you want a wonderful, easy, colourful cop-out, with all the benefits of a wildflower meadow but none of the hard work, go for a bed of annual cornfield flowers. Sow them (children like to do this) in ground that is as weed free as possible in early spring and in just a few months you'll have a colourful display of things like cornflowers, marigolds and corncockles. You can buy a cornfield annual mix from most seed suppliers.

Lawns: a wildlife desert

Lawns that are treated with chemicals or tightly mown all year are pretty atrocious for wildlife. The small piece of grass in Marc's garden is used as a wildflower area in the first half of the year and then cut like a lawn after that. This unusual management regime makes a big difference to wildlife.

Suppliers of wildfower seed

Emorsgate Wild Seeds
www.wildseed.co.uk

Suppliers of wildflower plugs

British Wild Flower Plants
www.wildflowers.co.uk

Really Wild Flowers of Dorset
www.reallywildflowers.co.uk

Landlife Wildflowers
www.wildflower.org.uk

▲ Hairy michaelmas daisy

▼ Wild golden rod   ▼ Wild marjoram

▼ Butterfly bush   ▼ Perennial sunflower

10

top plants for wildlife; recommended by Marc

1 Wild marjoram

2 Hairy Michaelmas daisy
'These are late summer- and autumn-flowering daisies. *Aster novae-angliae* and *Aster amellus* are the ones to get, they're not weedy or invasive.'

3 Wild golden rod
'but not invasive Canadian goldenrod, *Solidago virgaurea* is the one you want.'

4 Perennial sunflower
'*Helianthus* 'Lemon Queen' is a particularly pretty one.'

5 Single-flowered shrub and species roses.

6 Lavenders
'*Lavandula* x *intermedia* and other tall old-fashioned lavenders.'

7 Wild scabious

8 Globe thistles

9 Catmint

10 Butterfly bushes
'especially the orange-flowered *Buddleja* x *weyeriana*.'

Remember to leave everything to go to seed – for the birds.

MAKING A WILD BEE HOUSE

Bees need tunnels in dry wood to lay their eggs, so don't cut dead trees right down to the ground: the upright wood is better for the bees.

You can provide a manmade home for them as well. This house bee needs to be put up in the sunniest place you can find at about chest height.

- The basic ingredient is a chunk of wood – make sure it's not treated – with an angled cut on the top. Also shown here are a piece of wood to go on the top, to keep the rain off, and some screw eyes for fixing it to a wall, tree or fence.

- Drill lots of holes of different sizes as far into the chunk of wood as you can, up to a diameter of 8 millimetres.

- Attach a top to the sloping edge, enough to keep the rain off but not so much that it casts too much shade.

- Use screw eyes drilled into the wood at the back so the house can be easily hooked onto a fence.

Watch out for birds like woodpeckers who will try to get the bees' eggs out. Covering the bee house with wire netting or taking it to a sheltered place for winter – but it must be a cold place – will help. Put it back out in its sunny spot on 1 April when the following year's pollinators will start to emerge.

Bumble bees usually ignore nesting boxes, but heaps of dry grass or piles of dry wood will help them along.

Bee facts

- Bumble bees and honey bees live in groups, solitary bees don't (as their name indicates).

- There are 240 types of solitary bee in this country.

- These bees don't sting.

- Unlike honey bees, bumble bees and solitary bees only produce enough honey to feed their young and so they have no commercial value.

New perennial planting and wildlife

New perennial planting is a wonderful idea that is really taking off in gardens now and what Marc has done here is a variation on this. The idea is to use drifts of plants and grasses (as opposed to shrubs) that give movement, colour and a changing picture to the garden. With all their flowers, these plants are great for wildlife. Also you leave the plants standing through winter: the seed heads are a good source of food. Normally these perennial plantings are done on a big scale, but the same can be achieved, as here, in a smaller garden.

▲ A really stylish, modern bird bath from The Urban Garden.

◀ Get a child to put their apple into this feeder, by Frances Hilary, and their interest is immediately sparked every time a hungry bird starts to peck at it.

Cox & Cox ▶ stock a stylish and ready-made bee house to help bees overwinter in the garden.

◀ Ladybirds are wonderful little beasts to encourage into the garden and this tower, by Frances Hilary, is a perfect winter home for them.

Looking more ▶ like a dovecote than any ordinary bird box, this gothic nesting box with intricate woodwork and a copper top is by Frances Hilary.

Soft & Scented

DESIGN BRIEF
- **Something for the children but not a 'children's garden'**
- **Somewhere to eat outside in the shade**
- **A seat in the sun**
- **Storage**

FEATURES
- **Seating area with wooden uprights and wires across the top**
- **Hidden swing**
- **Mirrors on the rear fence**
- **Cobbles for transition from house to lawn**

The design for this small, city garden takes into account all of the points in the design brief and leaves a garden that is both beautiful and easy to live with. Claire Mee, the designer, has created a very soft garden with few hard edges and an air of the countryside about it. The hard lines that are here are used sparingly to give structure and balance to what could have been just a mass of planting. There is a central lawn that butts up to the house and planting along each side.

The main solid outline in the garden is the low wall protecting a shaded area to the rear for sitting and dining. The wall provides a visual divide to the garden and, when you're in the seating area, helps to create the feeling of being in a separate space. It also provides an entrance to the seating area over to the side of the garden.

'The house has a very modern extension but the clients didn't want an ultra-modern garden – they wanted a soft garden, full of flowers.'

Seating area At the rear of the garden there's a dining room with a large table. It's divided off from the rest of the garden by a low wall and upright posts. Wires are trained across the top of the area to hold the wisteria. All in all this creates an implied division across the garden: you can see through but there is a definite boundary, an enclosure, around the room at the bottom of the garden.

Swing A swing for the children is included but, because it uses natural materials and is surrounded by lots of planting, it doesn't jar; it becomes part of the garden.

Scented plants Scent is important in this semi-enclosed area. 'The scents will be much stronger here than out in the open so we didn't put too many competing flavours in or it would be overpowering,' says Claire. Wisteria, star jasmine and lavender provide the limited palette of summer scents.

Boundaries The boundaries have been covered with battens to provide consistency. There were, Claire says, five different types of fencing around the garden: 'You need to impose order but don't want to block anyone's light.' The battening gives a unified feel to the whole garden and looks more contemporary than plain trellis.

Evergreen structure It's a garden that blossoms into life in the summer with Campanulas, roses and Californian lilac, but it also has an underlying structure that anchors this abundance in summer and provides interest in winter. This garden is seen all through the year and the carefully positioned evergreen box balls, the evergreen olives and the hard landscaping will give it structure even in the depths of winter.

▲ **Very large wisteria plants** were purchased for the garden. It makes sense to do this for some of the planting, especially wisteria which is slow growing.

▲**There is no planting right** next to the house; the huge glass wall opens straight out onto lawn with only a narrow line of cobbles on the ground as a buffer.

▲ **The swing** provides hours of fun for the children without ruining the feel of the garden.

▲ **The eating area** is a magical place to be. In the evening, light is provided by candles overhead and on the table. Even in the daytime it's a lovely hideaway for the children. The seat also has an important practical use: under it is a storage area, large enough for the lawn mower.

▲ **3-millimetre stainless-steel wires,** bought from a local chandler, are stretched across the 'roof' of the dining area. The wisteria will grow along these but they aren't too imposing. Using these as opposed to wood, as Claire says, 'stops the structure being too dark, heavy and woody'.

'What has been created here is a very pretty, feminine garden that is balanced rather than symmetrical. The dining area to the rear of the garden, with its dappled shade and views back to the house, mirrors the large kitchen/dining room inside the house. This balance and structure convey a calm restfulness and order, which is a wonderful boon in a city garden.'

Design

It's tempting if you're designing your own garden to skimp on the borders – don't.
A good depth of planting as in this garden will make the whole garden more lush.
It will also make it easier to create hidden, secluded corners and surprises.

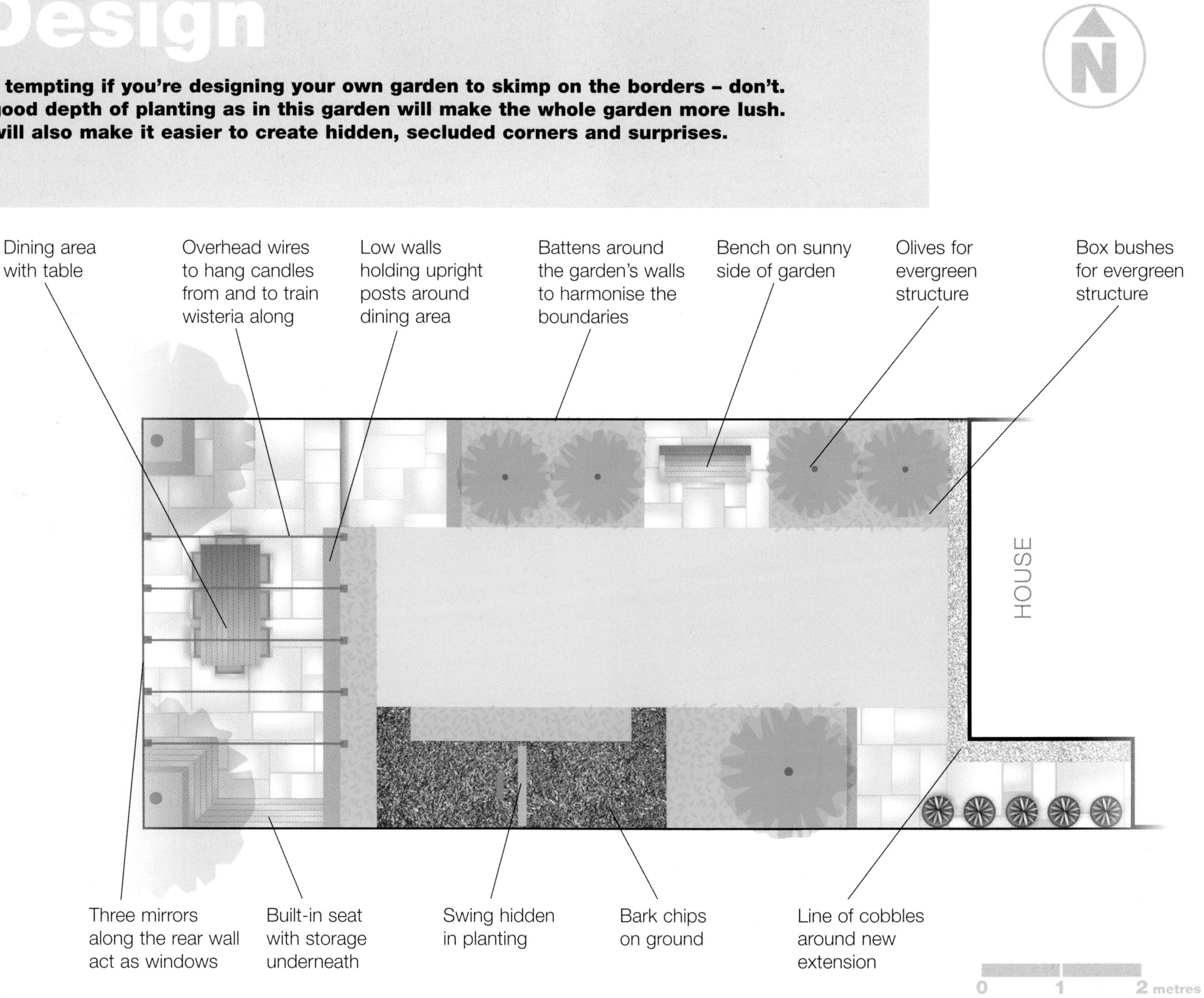

N

Dining area
with table

Overhead wires
to hang candles
from and to train
wisteria along

Low walls
holding upright
posts around
dining area

Battens around
the garden's walls
to harmonise the
boundaries

Bench on sunny
side of garden

Olives for
evergreen
structure

Box bushes
for evergreen
structure

HOUSE

Three mirrors
along the rear wall
act as windows

Built-in seat
with storage
underneath

Swing hidden
in planting

Bark chips
on ground

Line of cobbles
around new
extension

0   1   2 metres

7 steps to designing a city garden, from Claire Mee

Claire Mee has been designing gardens in London for many years and has met, and overcome, most of the problems they can throw up. Here are her 7 tips for creating the perfect small city garden.

1 Dividing up the garden

'People think that sectioning off areas will make the garden look smaller, but it doesn't. If you can't see the whole garden at once it will make it appear larger and give so much more interest.' In this garden the extra 'room' at the rear obscures the boundary and makes the whole garden seem bigger.

2 Boundaries

City gardens tend to inherit lots of different boundary fences and walls: 'It's like having a living room with different wallpaper on each wall – you need to make it more cohesive.' Claire uses battening and trelliswork to unify the boundaries and this instantly creates a cleaner look for the garden.

3 Light

Lack of light is often a problem in small gardens and they can appear dark and dingy. Bare red brick is a particularly bad offender: it sucks up light. Using light-coloured materials for trellis, painting walls and using render that can then be painted a light colour can all help to bounce around what light there is. Claire adds, 'You can also try using mirrors, as we have here, to increase light levels in small spaces.'

4 Materials

In a small space it's often more possible to use really good materials. 'The square metre cost won't be so prohibitive if there aren't too many square metres. We want our gardens to look as good in ten years' time as on the day they went in and more expensive materials will achieve that.' Natural materials are often the best and wear extremely well. Claire suggests Indian sandstone as a good, natural and reasonably priced paving.

5 Seating areas

Most gardens need a place to sit and Claire tries to put the seating area away from the house. 'If the seating area is next to the house the rest of the garden can become neglected, but with a seating area at the rear of the garden you have to make the journey through the garden. And when you're sitting there you look back through planting and greenery to the house. It feels like you're in the country.'

6 Specimen plants

Claire often uses large specimen plants. The wisterias and the olives in this garden were bought large. 'My clients often want an instant effect and in a city garden you can get that by putting in a few large plants, which can make all the difference in a small space.'

7 Wildlife

Planting of all sorts brings life into the garden: 'As soon as we've planted up a garden you can hear the buzz of insects and once you've got insects you'll get birds into the garden.' Claire's particularly keen on planting small fruit trees in city gardens, so that children can see how they develop from blossom and enjoy eating the produce and learn 'that fruit doesn't just come from supermarkets'.

Scented plants

Someone said to me that they don't get the point of scented plants: all this talk of wafting past lavender to release its smells doesn't work for them. They might be right, sometimes you have to get very close to the flowers to get the full effect – but this is exactly what children do and it's a joy for them to smell different things in the garden.

There are some plant scents that even our old noses can pick up, especially if they are in a semi-enclosed space. If you plant more than one and put them somewhere that you're going to get very close to, like by a seat or a doorway, you've got more chance of catching the scent.

Also think about scent throughout the year. Just as you might plan to have flowers coming at different times, so you can plan to have scents coming and going all year.

Spring

Burkwood osmanthus Large evergreen shrub with fragrant white flowers in spring. This is good if you need to fill a space or want to create a den inside a shrub by hollowing it out.

Armand clematis Evergreen climber with scented white spring flowers.

Perennial wallflower These are beautiful early flowering and fragrant plants.

Summer

Butterfly bush This might be a weed but the flowers smell of jam roly-poly and they attract butterflies by the hundred. One variety I like in particular is 'Black Knight', which has very dark purple flowers.

Lavender The quintessential summer scent. They do come in different shades of purple (and indeed in white) so ask for the shade you want; I always go for a really dark purple flower.

Roses For scent, climbing roses around a door or over an arch can't be beaten. 'Madame Alfred Carrière' is one of my favourites.

▲ Perennial wallflower

▲ Rose

Autumn

Oleaster Great for an evergreen hedge, this has tiny scented flowers in early winter.

Autumn flowering cyclamen A really lovely sweet smell, which gives the garden a great lift around September.

Clematis Can give a great show in the autumn. Clematis 'Wyevale' flowers in late summer and autumn with a very sweet scent.

Winter

Winter honeysuckle Not a pretty shrub, but its winter flowers smell beautiful.

Sweet box This is a member of the box family and can be used like box to add structure or make a hedge, but it has a wonderful advantage over normal box: it has incredibly strongly scented flowers in winter.

Witch hazel A small tree that has floppy yellow or orange flowers in winter with a distinctive smell. It prefers acid soil but can grow in alkaline soil, it just won't get very big.

▲ Cyclamen

▲ Witch hazel

SOME SMELLIES FOR CHILDREN

▲ Rosemary

▲ Pinks

▲ *Iris* 'Jane Phillips'

▲ Fennel

▲ Sweet peas

▲ Jasmine

▲ Personal touches such as these fishes by a pool add whimsy to a garden.

▲ The blue lights hanging from the wires in this garden are a lovely touch and add to the romantic appeal of the outside dining room.

Finishing touches

Finishing touches have little or nothing to do with gardening, they're about exterior decorating, making the space special and personal, and they can really make a garden.

▲ Candles look good in any nook or cranny.

▼ Even if you've no intention of using them, small bell jars like this look great.

▲ A watering can can be a beautiful thing.

▲ Small sculpture won't change the garden but adds interest

▲ Personalising an urn with a spray-painted star

▲ A mask on a pole stuck in the planting. Why? Why not?

▼ A metal wreath on a wall gives a highlight of silver to what might have been a dark area.

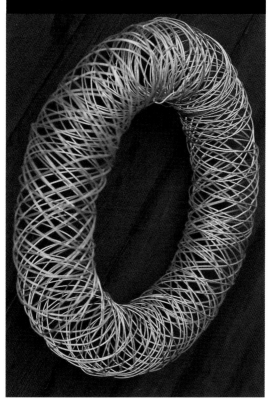

▲ Very traditional yet perfect for a modern garden, this beautifully made oak table and benches are from Arne Maynard.

◄ Just right for a modern garden this sleek stainless-steel water feature is from David Harber. (It lights up from within at night as well.)

If you have an ► apple tree the produce can be stored in this lovely traditional oak chest from Arne Maynard.

◄ From David Harber, this beautiful sphere of river-washed black stones is a work of art, and at night, light shines out from spaces between the pebbles.

RE have all sorts of ► practical and decorative bits and bobs for the garden and the home. These vintage watering cans are not only beautiful but useful as well – you can lazily leave them lying around in all weathers and they will look artfully placed, not just left out.

Contacts

Chapter 1

Designer

www.jamesleedesign.com
James Lee Landscape and Garden Design

Trellis

www.anthonydegrey.com
Bespoke architectural trellis and structures.
www.hillhout.com
Trellis and other garden products
www.metallicgarden.co.uk
Trellis and other metalwork for the garden

Woodwork

J.D. Wallis Joinery
01279 871 872
Thanks to John Wallis for advice on woodwork

Plants

www.randrsaggers.co.uk
Thanks to R&R Saggers nursery in Essex for providing trees and plants for the photography – along with wonderful advice

Chapter 2

Designers

www.delbuono-gazerwitz.co.uk
Tommaso del Buono and Paul Gazerwitz at Del Buono Gazerwitz

3

Chapter 3

Designers

www.acreswild.co.uk
*Debbie Roberts and Ian Smith
at Acres Wild Ltd*

Artificial grass

www.evergreensuk.com
For Lazy LawnTM – natural-looking artificial grass

4

Chapter 4

Designer

www.nashgardendesign.co.uk
Philip Nash Design Ltd.

Advice on garden floors

www.allseasonslandscape.co.uk
James Weston

5

Chapter 5

Designer

www.hdgardens.com
Helen Dooley Design

Willow structures and supplies

www.wildworks.org.uk
Carole Hockey at Wildworks

6

Chapter 6

Containers

www.capital-garden.com
For containers from terracotta and traditional to sleek and modern.

www.foxesboxes.co.uk
Creative window box and balcony dressing

www.privettint.co.uk
Metal containers, sculpture and water features for the garden.

7

Chapter 7

Designer

www.pdgardendesigns.co.uk
Paul Dracott at Agave

Lighting

www.ambienthome.co.uk
Funky modern furniture and lighting for inside and out

www.coxandcox.co.uk
Unusual homewares and gardenwares

www.theurbangarden.co.uk
Modern garden equipment, furniture and lighting

8

Chapter 8

Designer

www.clairemee.co.uk
Claire Mee Designs

Play equipment

www.coxandcox.co.uk
Unusual homewares and gardenwares

www.letterbox.co.uk
Quality toys and play equipment

www.urchin.co.uk
Toys, equipment and furniture for family living

Chapter 9

Designer

KFLA@blueyonder.co.uk
Karen Fitzsimon Landscape Architecture

Greenroof systems

www.greenfix.co.uk

Hideaways

www.egcc.biz
The English Garden Carpentry Company for custom-make hideaways

www.fletcherandmyburgh.co.uk
Unique seats

www.treehouselife.co.uk
Bespoke treehouses of all shapes and sizes.

www.urchin.co.uk
Toys, equipment and furniture for family living

www.wigwamsam.co.uk
For tepees large and small, to buy and to hire.

Plants

www.architecturalplants.com
Architectural plant suppliers

Chapter 10

Designer

www.paularyangardendesign.co.uk
Paula Ryan

11

Chapter 11

Designer

www.nashgardendesign.co.uk
Philip Nash Design Ltd.

Roof gardens

www.urbanroofgardens.com
Design and creation of stylish contemporary roof gardens

Green roofs

www.greenroof.co.uk
Blackdown Horticultural Consultants Limited, specialists in creating green roofs

12

Chapter 12

Sculpture and ornament

www.ambienthome.co.uk
Funky modern furniture and lighting for inside and out

www.gardentotems.co.uk
Unique, individual totem poles and other sculptures for the garden

grcarter@easynet.co.uk
George Carter – obelisks, seating and garden buildings

www.metallicgarden.co.uk
Trellis and other metalwork for the garden

www.steinworks.co.uk
Dramatic and elegant modern sculpture for gardens and interiors

13

Chapter 13

Attracting wildlife

www.coxandcox.co.uk
Unusual homewares and gardenwares

www.franceshilary.com
Unique garden gifts and horticultural products

www.theurbangarden.co.uk
Modern garden equipment, furniture and lighting

14

Chapter 14

Designer

www.clairemee.co.uk
Claire Mee Designs

Finishing touches

www.arne-maynard.com
Finely crafted traditional yet modern oak garden products by the writer and garden designer Arne Maynard

www.davidharber.com
Creators of both classical and contemporary sundials, sculptures and water features

www.re-foundobjects.com
Recycled, reclaimed and generally beautiful things for the garden and home